Whole Heart:

ONE WOMAN'S INCREDIBLE AND HEARTBREAKING JOURNEY FROM AFRICA TO AMERICA

BY

MICHELLE FELIX

Published by Michelle Felix

ISBN 978-0-57824-238-5

"At once heartbreaking and joyously uplifting, Whole Heart is an unflinching portrait of one woman's fight for self-discovery, opportunity, and hope. There is grace and possibility in even the bleakest of places, and I found it here, reading Michelle Felix's triumphant journey toward inner happiness."
- Angela Frazier (Multi-published author & editor).

"Her message of hope will resonate with everyone. Readers will be moved to tears by Michelle's struggles but also uplifted by her spirit and determination. Her story is ultimately one of forgiveness and love and faith in God that will inspire readers of all ages and from all walks of life."
- Heather Stockard

"A triumphant memoir that acknowledges pain and demands that we do more than just live in it."
- Samantha Hui (Independent Book Review)

"The author shares every aspect of her journey with readers, drawing them into her life and journey. Whole Heart will inspire, encourage, and give hope to many readers out there to create their own roads and walk along with them."
- Mamta Madhavan

"Whole Heart is the author's memoir as she chronicles her early life in South Africa and her eventual transition to life in The United States. Michelle Felix opens her whole heart as she traces the steps of a childhood that is almost impossible to fathom. Overall, this is well-told memoir.

- Readers' Favorite

ACKNOWLEDGMENT

Big thanks to the amazing Storyterrace team. A special thank you to Erin Stone, Christopher Armstrong, and the entire team, as well as Design Grade Design & Adeline Media, London. Without you guys, this journey would not be possible. www.storyterrace.com

I would also like to thank all the people who have helped and supported me in this journey, especially my husband Luis Felix, Stanley Munsamy, Dolly Perumal, Eddie Colon, and Wentworth-Shaw's.

CONTENTS

FOREWORD

I am grateful for the opportunity to tell my story, and to you, reader, for listening. It took me a great while to find the courage to put my experiences and the related emotions into words.

I believe that every one of us has a story to tell because our journeys are uniquely ours, and each season of our past shapes us and our future. Though no one can walk the same path you walk, the pain we feel - from rejection, abandonment, abuse, trauma, trials – is relatable across all walks of life.

My journey is one of pain but also healing. There were moments in my life when nothing around me reflected the dreams that God had put in my heart for a better life, a life where I could live in peace, purpose, and joy. One could say this is a story about a girl living in South Africa, hoping that America's legend as a place of possibility was true. Ultimately, this is a story of forgiveness, restoration, and finding joy on the other side of pain.

I dedicate this book to my unborn child. I hope one day when my son or daughter reads this book, they will know that obstacles, pain, and failures are part of life, but they do not control our future. I pray that my child, and you, dear reader, never stop believing in even the most seemingly impossible dreams. For it is our dreams and aspirations that give us the courage to face the fires of life.

1

LIFE IN AFRICA

Growing up in Durban, South Africa was special, with its beautiful coastlines and rich culture. Though apartheid was finally losing its influence, there was still evidence of its impact on the culture. I did not see the real-life situations of apartheid. However, I did experience the long-term effects of racial segregation and the inequality of human rights based on gender, race, and social status. Being of Indian descent, I've often felt in the middle, not white and not black.

As a young girl, I remember hearing President Nelson Mandela speak of South Africa as a "rainbow nation," and it resonated with me. "Madiba," as he was often called in his motherland because he truly was the good father of the nation, longed to see equality among the different races that called Africa home. His words had weight: here was a man who went from prisoner to president and endured persecution in hopes that his homeland would rise above apartheid, ushering in freedom and equality. He refused the mantra of an "eye-for-an-eye" instead choosing to lead with love. Mandela changed the country's very soul, giving the people of Africa hope for a better future. His love and hope were contagious.

Growing up, my dad often reminded me of how lucky I was to live in the new South Africa, and that sentiment has stayed with me. My granny shared a story of when my dad was eight years old and ran in to use the white-only toilets because black-only toilets were full, and urgency had struck. Granny witnessed a policeman hit my dad with a stick and throw him out of the bathroom. My granny pleaded for forgiveness from the policeman fearing for her son's life.

There was nothing fancy about growing up in Africa. People worked hard to provide for their families. My mum and dad both came from humble beginnings and a legacy of resilient and hard workers. My great grandfather on my mother's side came to South Africa during the migration of indentured Indian labor in the British colonies. At the age of fourteen, he labored in the cane fields and worked his way up to become a small-scale sugarcane grower. European big-scale growers owned the good farming land, and unsuitable land was leased or sold to non-white, small-scale growers like my grandfather. His land was in a valley, only accessible by footpath and too rocky for tractors. However, the land was blessed with a small river that provided crystal clear water and never dried up even in the harshest droughts.

My mother, Subbammah "Gonum" Chetty Munsamy,

grew up in Kranskloof in a modest, but accommodating, farmhouse occupied by her parents and six children. There was no electricity and evening studies were done by light from a paraffin lamp. Paraffin was an essential and precious commodity, and it was carefully managed as was every resource on the farm. Thanks to my grandfather's ingenuity, the farmhouse was one of the first homes in the region to have running water and a toilet. My grandfather was a brilliant and highly industrious man, building a functioning farm with running water literally with his own hands. It would have been such an honor to have met him.

All the children helped on the farm, and mum's daily chores included fetching firewood and water and helping in the vegetable garden. They'd also farmed bananas, which provided money to buy weekly groceries. The bananas were loaded into a donkey-drawn cart and hauled to the bus station where they were loaded onto the bus headed to the small town of Shakaskraal about 50 kilometers north of Durban on the main north coast road.

The Indian community in Kranskloof, like all Indian communities in the British colony of Natal at the time, started a school. The first school met under the shade of a tree, and the first teacher was Mr. V. N. Naidoo, who married mum's second eldest sister. The community combined resources to build a proper school building which still stands today. In the days of apartheid, it was an Indian only school, but is now open to all.

My grandfather was the "serviceman" for the local school, fixing whatever needed to be fixed. The school's water supply depended solely on rainwater, and the roof gutters and water tanks frequently needed essential maintenance. It is amazing to think of all that my grandfather built and attended to in order to build out this small farm community. As the decades wore on, the economies of scale made small scale farming incredibly challenging, and my grandfather eventually sold the farm and moved away.

My mother and her youngest sibling, Stanley, attended this school up until grade six and were the only two in the family who attended school. The local school could not accommodate all the pupils, so the children were split between morning and afternoon classes. Stanley attended in the mornings, and mum would walk him there every day and then stay for her afternoon sessions. It was a long walk to school, and the two siblings would set out at six-thirty in the morning and not return home until just before dinner. Mum helped mentor Stanley and encouraged him in his education. He would later become a chemical engineer.

After obtaining good grades in primary school, mum went to Stanger Indian High School. She had boarded with her older sister in Shakaskraal and traveled by bus to Stanger. At that time, girls in the farming community were not encouraged to attend high school, but since my mother was a very dedicated student, she was afforded more educational opportunities. During the apartheid era, the preferred career for young Indian women was teaching or nursing. Completing studies in these areas came with a guaranteed job after graduation. This was significant, since these opportunities were reserved for white people under the Government's job reservation policy. Mum enrolled in St. Aidan's Mission Hospital in Durban with the intent of becoming a nurse.

Just once per month, as the journey was far from simple, my mother would go home to visit her family on the farm. She had to catch a train or bus on Friday from Durban to Shakaskraal and another bus to Kranskloof; she then made the return trip on Sunday. On one of mum's early visits, she'd brought a battery-operated Sanyo radio with a record player. Because the farmhouse was in a valley, the radio reception was not good, but the record player was a marvel. This was around 1965, and pop music was the rave. On each of her subsequent monthly visits she would bring home a new "7 single" or a music album.

My mother secured a nursing job at St. Aidan's Hospital, and as a result of her compassion and hard work she was promoted to the maternity section and became a head nurse. Because my mum worked at St. Aidan's Hospital, several babies in the family were born in this hospital. My cousins Ricky and Jo Anne and many others were born under my mum's attentive care and watchful eyes.

My father, Somasunthus "Joey" Pillay, was the eldest child in his family with seven siblings. He only completed his schooling through junior high school. In stories of his childhood, I'd never heard any mention of his father. However, I know that when my father was just a child himself, he took on jobs to earn money to help ensure his mother and siblings had food and necessities. He worked part-time delivering newspapers, sold homemade samosas in the street, and washed dishes at The Admiral Hotel. His mother depended on him for provisions and assistance with his siblings. My granny always had a soft spot for dad; he could do nothing wrong in her eyes. Understanding his childhood, and the struggles he'd endured, brought to light her unconditional love for him. His resilience and compassion to provide for his family as a child had always amazed me.

My father left home at fourteen, I was told due to problems at home, and lived with his aunt and uncle in Shakaskraal, the same town where my mother was attending nursing school. He took a job as a bartender at his uncle's hotel and learned the hotel business' logistics from administration duties to running hotel operations. Though he was under the supervision of his uncle and aunt, he was effectively on his own at a very young age.

My fondest and most lasting memory of growing up in Africa was the unity among the people. Communities would come together from all walks of life to celebrate special occasions or mourn losses. There was a united spirit of unity amongst the people as if every pain or joy I'd felt was shared with the entire community. We were one in spirit and, even in the times when I could not see it tangibly, unity was sowed into the earth of the nation.

My humble beginnings in Africa made me realize how the simple things in life gave me the most joy: time with family and friends, playing board games with my cousins, and simple food made in the humblest of homes. The farmlands in the region were so free and open, and I remember the joy of visiting my Aunt Panjalay's farm in Glendale as a young girl. Each visit was packed with adventure: playing in the beautiful green pastures, swimming in waterfalls, and eating meals like outside fire chicken curry with handmade roti. After sunset, we would light paraffin lamps and talk until late into the night.

Durban (also known as Kwa-Zulu Natal) is the land of the Zulu Nation, and the deep roots and spirit of the Zulu people and their culture are prominent there. To many like me, who found a new nation to call their homeland, Africa will always be their true home. The story of Africa is one of hope, even amid chaos. The people of Africa are strong, fearless, and courageous, always hoping for a brighter tomorrow, no matter the circumstances they face. As a nation that fought for a better future and continues to fight for a better tomorrow, the people of Africa instilled in me the power of perseverance in times of struggle. And that is a fight I know well.

"May your choices reflect your hopes, not your fears."
- Nelson Mandela

2

THE BEGINNING, FOR ME

I was born on June 26, 1982, in Durban, South Africa, to a loving family. My aunt once told me the doctors had to induce labor for my mother because I had grown too big in her womb. As a result, I'd entered the world as a premature baby, yet overweight baby. I am told I was the largest premature baby ever born in that hospital.

My early arrival meant my lungs were not properly developed, and I've struggled with asthma from the time I was born. I would have severe attacks that would keep me in the hospital for weeks at a time. Because my attacks were so unpredictable, I had to take my nebulizer with me everywhere.

My mother, being a nurse, knew exactly how to care for me. I'd depended on her greatly in those times of weakness. Mum had a big oxygen tank and medications for me at home to avoid hospital trips, but I still ended up there four or five times a year. I could feel her frequent worry over my illness. I am sure I seemed so fragile in her eyes, and in many ways I was.

The attacks were frightening, but mum's love and care always reassured me. Once, when I was around eight years old, my family – dad, mum, my sister, and I – were sitting downstairs in our living room, watching television together. I went upstairs to get my homework from the room I had shared with my sister, and suddenly I just stopped breathing. I couldn't get air. I had no breath to call my family and no energy to crawl to help. I remember laying on the floor in the room praying that someone would come to help me. I didn't really know who I was praying to, but I cried out in my soul. The next thing I knew, I heard my mother's voice.

"Where is she?"

She found me, gave me oxygen, and then carried me to my bed. She stayed with me until I could breathe on my own, and then my dad carried me to the car to take me to the hospital again.

In primary school, I struggled academically. Mum would spend long hours teaching me basic counting and word skills. Unfortunately, my report card showed little to no improvement. My parents worried continuously about my slow learning. Parent/teacher nights were always a disappointment for my parents. An occasional stutter, brought on by nerves, caused me great embarrassment during speeches in front of the class. I remember my classmates laughing at me as I spoke, and my teacher reprimanding them. Eventually, my teacher allowed me to perform my speeches to her only. She was kind to me.

My sister was the smart one, and beautiful, too. She excelled in all subjects and even won beauty pageants in school. She was in newspapers after she won the Miss Saree contest. I was immensely proud to call her my sister and bragged about her to my classmates.

The worry my parents carried over my health and academic struggles burdened me. I was frequently bullied, and my classmates would call me "fatty" and "slow" since I could not participate in sports. I had tried taking on a few sports at school, hoping I would find a hidden talent and a place to fit in, but my shortness of breath due to my asthma made most sports difficult except for one: of all things, arm wrestling! Despite my premature birth, I was a big girl for my age, and I could win against most boys, as well as my older cousins (much to their chagrin). I was strong and mighty in my own way, I suppose.

My parents loved me with all my weaknesses and always believed in me. They would praise and encourage me for the smallest things, and it made me so happy to see them smile and their worry wane, even if just temporarily. Though I was not an achiever in primary school, my parent's love was more than enough for me. Their approval was all I needed to be happy.

"Where there is love there is life."
- Mahatma Gandhi

3

MY FAMILY

My family lived in a modest council house; it was government housing afforded to them due to my mother's job as a midwife. My sister and I shared one of the two bedrooms and slept in bunk beds. There was nothing extravagant about it, but when I think of home, this small and cozy space is what comes to mind.

Our home was in a predominantly Indian suburb called Overport that was within a Muslim community. When the Muslim prayers would come over the loudspeaker, dad would quiet my sister and me and instruct us to be respectful. Dad taught us that you do not need to understand another man's religion, but you must always respect it. This is a lesson that has stayed with me. Growing up in a country with eleven official languages and receiving the important lesson of respecting all religions has enabled me to embrace and appreciate the uniqueness of others.

Dad was a Christian but rarely attended church, and my mother was Hindu, and very dedicated to her Hindu practices. She would let me help her light the worship lamp in her small prayer space. I did not understand this sacred practice, but it felt good to know a higher power was watching over us. I truly felt comfortable with both of my parents' chosen religions. Occasionally, my sister and I would go to church with dad, but for the most part, we kids were left to decide for ourselves what spiritual path, if any, we would follow.

Mum worked the night shift as a midwife, and dad worked during the day in private security. He also served as a reserve police officer for our community. They worked extremely hard for our family, looking to give all of us a good life.

I loved to see my mother in her crisp, white nursing uniform. In South Africa, nurses wear different colored epaulets on the shoulders of their uniforms to indicate their specialization or role. As a registered midwife, my mother's epaulets were the most vibrant shade of green. The way she carried herself was as inspiring as the work she did, helping to bring life into the world on almost a daily basis. She loved her job, and she had worked so hard, rising above her circumstances to earn it.

Dad first met my mother at a dance. Being a big city Casanova working in a metropolitan hotel, he swept my modest, farm girl mother off her feet. He was her first love, and he became her world. She was beloved by dad's many siblings, especially his sisters, and she mentored them in child rearing when they were new mothers. Mum encouraged dad to finish his education and helped him complete high school. Education was always a priority for my mother.

Dad was a vivacious people person, and everywhere we went people would want to stop to chat with him. Mum, although was stunningly beautiful, was by contrast very reserved. Where dad was boisterous, mum was mostly quiet and did not say much, but she had a discreet, almost hidden strength. She was also the stronger earner between them, and even the very home we lived in was due to her job.

Growing up, I was definitely a daddy's girl, and I was very tomboyish. I think after having my sister, who was five years older than me, he had hoped for a son, and he sometimes treated me as one. I happily avoided dresses, mostly wearing caps and shorts instead.

I didn't see much of my parents because they worked frequently. My dad would drop my sister and me off at school in the morning. When we got home in the afternoon, Mum would be resting, waking around 4:00 p.m. to see us before getting ready for work. Dad would return home from his job and, without coming into the house, mum would go out and jump in his car, and he would drive her to work. She never drove. Although she had a license, my father never allowed her to drive. She didn't do anything on her own except for work. She did not even shop for feminine products; if she needed anything, dad would go get it.

Though my parents were often unavailable, and my sister was engrossed in older girl interests, I had my beloved dogs to keep me company. An unfortunate result of missing so much school due to my frequent hospital stays was that I didn't really have friends. But our dogs were my absolute best friends. We had three amazing boxers: Mash, Tiffany, and Jock. After school, I would race home, throw my school bag on the kitchen table, and run outside to play with them, not even stopping to change out of my school uniform. Time with my dogs was pure joy. We would play all afternoon together.

Dad trained the boxers as if they were police dogs. Crime in South Africa was rampant, and this was his way of protecting us when he was away at work. They were amazing dogs, and my family still talks about how intelligent and special they were.

I have happy memories of our time at the council house. I remember mum cooking the most amazing curries with saffron, which was very expensive and an indulgence in our humble home. When my dad would cook, it would consist of Americanized meals like hot dogs, burgers, and sandwiches. I loved it all. On weekends, we would go out to eat and spend time together.

Since my parents both came from large families, we had many relatives nearby, and we celebrated holidays together as most families do. On Christmas Day, we would go to my paternal grandmother's house, and dad's siblings and my cousins would all join. I loved spending time with my cousins; cooking curries, breaking bread, and lots of laughter. Our Christmas lunch tradition was a spicy crab curry. Eating crab curry with your hands did take skill, but it was fun and messy, especially with everyone's faces turning red from the curry. After lunch, we exchanged gifts. I never understood why, but every year I was given a tea set even though some of my cousins received fancier gifts. My granny had her favorites, and my sister was one of them.

I don't remember my parents showing much affection to my sister and me, but they expressed their love in small moments. My parents were goal-driven, and I admired their hard work and dedication to give us the best life possible. Dad tried to open his own business, and mum worked on getting another specialization in nursing while we were growing up. They've always provided for us, and when I was sick and needed help, they were always there.

"Never complain about what your parent couldn't give you. It was probably all they had."

\- Rafia Azeez

4

LIGHT TURNS TO DARKNESS

My parents were so proud when they could purchase us a nice, new house in Phoenix, an Indian suburb northwest of Durban central. 109 Cherrywood Road was the appropriately charming address of our beautiful new home. Unlike the modest council house, this new home was so beautiful and fancy, especially from a nine-year-old's perspective. The kitchen had granite countertops and shiny appliances. I had my own room; and we had a large yard where I could play with my dogs.

The one thing that stood out the most was the stone design chimney. I had never seen a chimney before except for when my family would settle in to watch American movies together. It was not a real, functioning chimney, just a fancy display. Dad designed the front yard into a botanical garden with colorful lighting and garden ornaments.

The new house was night and day compared to our council house, but it would come to be that the simpler home held far more happiness for my family. It was as if the new environment created problems overnight. Mash, being the oldest of our three boxers, died shortly after the move. I think the transition was just too much for him. I was heartbroken. I remember holding his lifeless body and pleading to my father to let him stay. My father tried to make me feel better by telling me Mash was now in "dog heaven." Losing him, my best friend, was the first painful loss I'd grieved, and it was far too soon for both of us.

My parents often fought, and the tension seemed to hang in the air. There were no more goodbye kisses between mum and dad before he left for work. I remember her waiting in worry when dad was not home in time to drive her to her job. A couple of days, he did not come home at all, and mum had to miss work, which she never did. Even on his days off, dad started staying away from our home. He didn't seem like the same vivacious person anymore.

Mum and dad's arguments would frighten me, and I would hang on to my dogs, Tiffany, and Jock. I could not understand what was happening, and no one explained it to me, which left many questions for me as a nine-year-old girl, who was so dependent on her parents. I was convinced that every fight would be their last and that things would then go back to how they were before. I understand now that the change in their relationship was gradual, but as a child, it seemed that my family home went from happy to hostile almost overnight.

As I became more and more fearful of the situation with my parents, my asthma began acting up with more frequency. I didn't want to go to school or even to play. In the absence of anyone to tell me otherwise, I couldn't help but wonder if it was somehow my fault; something I had done to make dad not like his life with us anymore. I didn't understand at the time that there was another woman, I only saw pain and sorrow overwhelm my mother. Her happiness had faded. She rarely ate, and she stayed alone in her room most of the time.

I clearly remember the day it all fell apart. Dad was trying to walk away from mum as she held on to his hand. He turned to her and said, "I just don't want this anymore. This is not for me. I don't feel the same about you, and I just can't go on like this anymore."

Mum pleaded with him, eager to change, "to do better." Anything to get him to stay. I remember the sorrow on her face and the anger on my father's. My asthma came on quickly, and I passed out, waking to see the ceiling fan spinning above me and hearing my mother's strained and tearful voice.

"Look what you've done! You're going to kill my child!"

I had never heard my gentle mother speak so assertively and with such intensity. Dad grabbed me up, and they both rushed me to the hospital where I had stayed for a week. Mum came to my bedside every day.

When we returned home, my father had not left, but there was another shift in the atmosphere. I was so young, but I sensed and observed it all. The arguments had stopped, but they barely spoke to each other. Mum changed her night shift to day shift, and in the mornings, we would all load up in the car and leave together. I vividly recall the tension during the ride on our way to school before dropping my mother off at the hospital. No one spoke, and dad did not say a word to mum not even a simple "goodbye" or "have a nice day" as she left the car.

I don't know if she was aware of it, but mum's sadness was so evident all in her demeanor. She was alive but not living. Although she was with us physically, emotionally she was dead. Only occasionally would she even direct a smile toward me. How I loved and missed the warmth my mother's smile could bring. My dad was never home. He dropped us at school, and we would only see him again right before bed. Mum reasoned to us that it was because he was working overtime. Our family weekends together slowly began to fade. With dad rarely home, my sister hanging out with friends, and mum secluded in her room, I was on my own, grateful to have my dogs to keep me company.

One night, dad came home with freshly caught fish. I hadn't even known that he had gone fishing. He was smiling proudly as he called us to the kitchen. We sat around the table like a family again as dad cleaned the horrible smelling fish. He then fried it and served it to us. Boy, did we enjoy it! Sharing food, space, and laughter over dad's messy cooking with mum happily trying to help him. There was so much happiness. I felt like all the good memories had been revived, and we loved and wanted each other again. I still can so clearly recall dad and mum smile at each other; it reminded me of a Hindi movie scene with a girl and boy hiding behind a tree smiling at each other.

For the first time in a long time, I had felt whole again. Seeing my parents, and our family, together at that moment made me happier than anything in the world. Unfortunately, it would only last for a moment. If I had known it was to be our last happy memory as a family, I would have done everything in my power to make that night last forever.

"Many unforgettable moments are worth more than a lifetime of memories."

\- Michelle Felix

5

HER FIRST ATTEMPT

A few weeks later, with the palpable tension and obvious distance between my parents reinstated, mum made her first suicide attempt. Dad and I had gone to Clicks Pharmacy for a few items he needed; I always loved to tag along with him everywhere he went. When we returned home, the house was strangely silent, and her bedroom door was locked.

Dad began banging on the door and calling out to her, "Gonum, Gonum, open the door!" There was no response. As dad continued to bang and call to her, I went outside to peer through their bedroom window to see if she was there. I saw her lying on the bed, unconscious. I ran back to the house, crying out to my father, "She's sick! You need to break down the door!"

He broke open the door, and there was my mum; her arm hanging awkwardly off the corner of the bed and syringes scattered around on the floor. Dad dragged her lifeless body to the car, her head falling and bobbing as he moved her. They made it to the hospital in time for her to be saved, though she stayed there for several weeks recovering.

I remember sitting by mum's bedside in the hospital, and telling her, "Mum, you cannot leave me. Who will take care of me when I get sick? I can't live without you. I cannot make it without you." Perhaps it was a selfish thought when mum was struggling so much herself, but I desperately needed to feel safe. My mother was my security when it came to my own health.

It always struck me that when dad drove her to the hospital that day, though he could have driven to any of the nearby hospitals in town, he chose to drive her to Phoenix Hospital where she had worked. Her coworkers saw her in this terrible state. They knew it was an overdose, and perhaps were even suspicious that she had taken the medication from the hospital. This would taint the one place where my mother felt strong, admired, and honored. The darkness she was experiencing at home had been exposed.

The day we were able to bring mum home from the hospital, I was so happy. However, she was withdrawn; her face was empty and sad. She was losing her marriage and happy home, and now she had lost the dignity she drew from her nursing job. She would continue to work, but she lost her twinkle after that. Even then, I still somehow believed that things would get better for our family and go back to how they were.

Looking back, I wonder if the overdose was an attempt to ensure my father would stay. Her suicide attempt had the opposite effect, and dad's treatment toward her worsened. It saddened me to see my dad show no compassion toward his wife and the mother of his children as she wallowed in pain. She needed a shoulder to cry on. She needed to know the man she had loved for seventeen years still wanted her to exist. She was weak and fragile, while my dad was ready to start a new life. Mum was beautiful inside and out, smart, humble, and grace filled. My dad could do the worst, and she would forgive him. I wish mum could have seen herself through my eyes, she would have realized how amazingly beautiful and strong she was.

I still struggle to understand why dad could not find just one reason to stay. I wrestled with this thought many times, but I never had the courage to ask him. How do you completely stop loving someone after seventeen years of marriage? How do you detach from any feeling or need to care for and support someone at the weakest point in their life? How can you just walk away, and not once look back?

I can only imagine the pain weighing on my mum's soul, suddenly unloved by the only man she's ever loved. Knowing her gentle nature, she probably looked at herself as being the problem. Maybe she felt she was not pretty enough or good enough for him, or that she had somehow changed and that's what caused this change in him. I know my mum would have done anything for dad to stay. Absolutely... anything!

"Always remember, you're more than enough."

\- Unknown

6

SEPARATION

It was only a few days after bringing mum home from the hospital that dad told her he wanted a divorce. She was still weak and healing, and when she heard his demand, she asked him, "Can we take a break instead?" She had tried everything to keep their marriage together, or at least to delay the inevitable. She was so dependent on him, she truly felt she could not survive without him. They decided on a six-month separation. My parents stood in front of my sister and I, and my dad spoke to us stone-faced.

"Choose who you want to go with."

My sister went straight over to dad. I wanted to go with him too, but my nine-year-old logic reasoned that it would not be fair for me to choose him, too. And I was afraid to leave mum on her own. It happened so fast, this life-altering moment. I didn't know it at the time, but that represented the end of my parents' seventeen-year marriage, and one of the last times my family would be together.

By South African law, mum was entitled to the house,

and it was her earnings that enabled our family to have it, but she didn't take it. She didn't care about the financials or much of anything else; she had lost all hope and wanted to escape. We packed up and moved in with her older sister and her daughter in Tongaat.

The living arrangements at my aunt's house were tight. Though the home was small, there was lots of room to play outside, and I liked the traditional look of her home. I had to change schools, and my new school was within walking distance from my aunt's house. At this school, I wasn't teased as much. Because my mother did not have a car, getting to work was a challenge. Our house in Durban had been twenty minutes to her job, but Phoenix Hospital was an hour or more from Tongaat. She took a taxi there and back every day.

Dad would come to visit briefly about once a week. He would ask me how I was doing, as well as if mum was doing okay. I'd tell him the truth, like a child would, that mum was sad and not eating much. He would assure me that she would be alright, saying that she "just needed time." He didn't seem concerned. I would tell him how much I missed the dogs and ask him to bring them on his next visit, but he never did.

My sister never joined my dad on the visits either, and it broke my mother's heart to be away from her child and to think her daughter didn't want to see her. Mum and dad would usually talk outside before he left, and I always hoped for reconciliation; that we could come home, and all be together again. But although I couldn't hear what they were saying, I could feel the tension and see their expressions turn angry. Sometimes my dad would just walk off in the middle of them talking and leave. Relatives told me he would ask her for money on these visits and threaten to take me from her if she didn't give it to him.

I think my dad felt the separation was a burden and only delaying what he really wanted. He was already with another woman. I once heard that during this time, he left my sister with one of my aunts and brought this new woman to our family home. I don't know whether mum knew about this, but her disposition continued to deteriorate. She would sit in her room, and listen to Michael Bolton sing, "How Am I Supposed to Live Without You" on repeat.

I tried my best to make my mother happy. One day at school, I had received a good report that was rare for me as I was still pretty slow academically. I was usually among the bottom three in the class, but this report had me in the top fifteen. When I showed her, a fleeting smile came over her weary face, but not much more.

We looked forward to our occasional visits to Durban to visit mum's friend Priscilla, a fellow nurse. She had three daughters just a bit older than me, and it was so fun to be around other children. Priscilla's house was just fifteen minutes from the hospital which meant a break from long taxi trips for my mother. The mothers would go to work together, and the kids would stay home and play.

I liked that mum had someone to talk to, and I could see she seemed less burdened when we were there. Priscilla and her family genuinely cared about us. We even had our own room there, mum and me. The warm and lively household made for a welcomed change. I felt mother and I were happy on those visits, and I was always eager to go.

"There are possibilities wherever hope lives."
- Michelle Felix

7

IF ONLY I HAD STAYED

One weekend in July, a few weeks after my eleventh birthday, Priscilla invited us for the weekend. We arrived on a Friday, and off mum and Priscilla went to work. On Saturday morning, Priscilla invited mum and me to join her family at a Zululand wedding, suggesting the change of scenery would be nice. Mum said she didn't feel like going, but it sounded like such fun; I very much wanted to enjoy the wedding with the other girls. Priscilla asked if she could bring me with them. Mum turned to her and said, "I don't think it's a good idea. Let Michelle stay here with me."

They set out to leave, but I came to my mother and pleaded for her to let me go. "Please don't go. Just stay with me," she said. I asked her three times to let me go with them, and all three times she said "no" to the point where she was nearly begging me to stay. After a moment, she came to me and told me I could go to the wedding. To my delight, she gave me R50 to take with me. I kissed her goodbye, and we were off.

It was a long drive to Zululand, and we had planned to stay overnight. Once we arrived, I became very agitated and started behaving very contrarily. It was unlike me, but for some reason I could not get a hold of myself. My stinky behavior caused Priscilla's family to change plans and, so instead of staying overnight, we headed back to Durban immediately after the wedding. As much as I had wanted to go to the wedding, now I was so glad to be going back to my mother.

As we got closer to Priscilla's house, I had asked if we could stop, so I could use the R50 mum had given me to bring her a treat. I bought a chicken rounder from KFC and a Cadbury's whole nut chocolate bar; I could not wait to see her and present them to her. I raced through the front door and headed straight for the stairs keeping my gaze downward to make sure I didn't miss a step and drop the treats.

As I reached the top, I lifted my eyes and first saw my mother's feet hovering above the ground. I looked up and saw her hanging with a belt around her neck, her skin completely blue. While staring at my mother's face in complete shock and confusion, I instantly had an asthma attack and fell down the stairs.

When I woke up, my dad and other family members were there. I remember police officers standing around the room taking notes with a large black bag in the background. I remembered my last sight before passing out from the asthma attack. I asked Dad, "Where's Mommy?" To me, the only possibility was that she would be okay. She had survived the first attempt, and she would survive this. Dad and the other relatives told me she was at the hospital, and that it would be okay.

Dad took me to his sister's house, where my sister was staying. I had not seen her since mum, and I left our home in Durban after the separation. This was not the reunion I would have hoped for, as my sister was the one to tell me the truth. "Mommy's not here anymore," she said. I could not process these words. I kept saying, "That's not true! That's not true!" I was angry at her for saying this, and my mind kept going to the last image of my mother, hanging in our bedroom at Priscilla's house.

In the days leading up to the funeral, and even when our family held the Indian tradition of sitting around the coffin, her death didn't hit me. I remember thinking, "Why is mum in this box?" I didn't want to believe that it was her. Her family made sure she was in her beautiful nurse uniform. As my mother's coffin went into a slide, where the furnace was, one of my relatives told me to say goodbye. I could not cry or feel any emotion at all.

We drove to the ocean to scatter her ashes, and I felt sadness and fear creeping in as I began to accept the truth that perhaps my mum truly was gone. My uncle told me I needed to throw her ashes into the ocean. He said to me, *"Your mother is at rest now, she is at peace. You have to do this and set her free."* At that moment, when I tossed the ashes into the ocean, I knew it was her, and that she was truly gone.

Accepting the reality of losing mum was heartbreaking, but the act of releasing her ashes into the sea gave me some sense of peace. I did not want her to leave me, but I was there with her in her last few weeks, even if they were filled with emptiness and sorrow. The depths of her pain must have been devastating to cause her to inflict such suffering upon herself. I could not save my beautiful mother, but watching her ashes dissolve into the waves, I could not help but think that perhaps she was happy now.

Once the funeral was over, it was as if mum had been erased. No one talked about her. Maybe it was too difficult to handle or, perhaps, it was due to the shame of how she died. I wish just one person could have talked to me about her and explained to me why she was gone. She wrote a lengthy letter before she took her life. I never got to see it, but I'm told she wrote that she couldn't live without my dad and asked that the family take care of her girls and make sure that we stayed together. I've tried to retrieve the letter, unsuccessfully. Supposedly it was kept by the police in mum's file upon her death. I hope I can read it one day.

Following her death, my mother's family was furious with dad and despised him. Conflict even broke out at the funeral; My uncle was so angry at dad and blamed him for her death. As a result, I was cut off from my mother's family almost immediately after the funeral. My sister and I stayed with our aunt for a while, I still wonder if it was during this time that dad held the wedding to his second wife that I would see only in photos years later.

I will never know what made dad walk out on my mum. I do know the decisions we make in life can have tremendous consequences for the people we love. I realize how even just one moment changed our lives forever. I can hear mum pleading with dad, "Let us try to work it out for the children's sake." How different things would be if dad had tried. Instead, a marriage of seventeen years ended, and the lives of two children were forever changed, by my father's irrational decisions. Now I understand that in her dark hours, mum was crying out for help on the inside but was too scared to admit it. She closed herself up, and the pain consumed everything inside of her that might have given her hope. Every reason to live was blinded by pain and suffocated by fear. She honestly believed that without my dad, her life had no meaning.

My mother's love for her children never changed; that was never in question. But she fought a battle in her mind that she just could not escape. I know in my heart there must have been times where she wanted to live, but ultimately her pain was too deep to find peace.

"Place your hand over your heart, can you feel it?
That is called purpose. You are alive for a reason,
so don't ever give up."

- Unknown

8

UNWELCOMED, UNWANTED

After a while, dad came to retrieve me from my aunt's house, but my sister stayed behind. I moved back into our home in Phoenix, where dad was now living with his new wife. At least I was finally back with my beloved dogs, Tiffany and Jock.

I had so much pain and so many unanswered questions bottled up inside of me. Why couldn't we have just stayed a family back in Phoenix? Why would mum leave me at just ten years old? At times, I hated her for what she did, leaving me at such a young age, knowing I needed her, and that I chose to go with her over my dad. Still, I never regretted that choice. I was able to be with her to the end, and I may be the only person who truly acknowledged the depths of her sorrow.

With no one to talk to, I dealt with my pain by eating. I rarely even spoke. It had to have been clear to my dad how emotionally unstable I was. I needed counseling or support, but no one in my traditional Indian family believed in mental health treatment. People were expected to pick up the pieces and move on. I truly felt hopeless.

I could tell dad was making efforts to be supportive. He was more affectionate during that time than I had ever remembered him being. Though he never expressed any regret or remorse over my mother's death, I think he felt burdened about all that led up to it, and that I was the one to find her. He would kiss me on the cheek and say, "Goodnight, baby."

My stepmom despised everything about me. In front of my dad, she would act with some consideration toward me. But when he was away at work, it was completely different. I had no emotional strength to protest her treatment. When I came home from school, she would give me nothing more than dry bread and curry gravy, though the cupboards were filled with food. My stepmom never wanted me in the house when dad wasn't there, so I spent most of my time outside with my dogs. She loathed them as much as she did me. I was so numb inside you could have thrown stones at me and I wouldn't have budged. Perhaps the only emotion I felt at that time was fear of my stepmom.

I was back in my former school, but I was not motivated to learn. I did not want friends because I did not want to talk about my family. I would spend my lunch break in the bathroom, and constantly walked with my head down. When I had my first menstruation, I was so confused about what was going on with me; and I honestly thought I was dying. When I told my stepmom, she shrieked at me to go to my room and not come out. When dad came home, he took me to my aunt's house, and she explained it to me.

My stepmom had a list of chores for me every day, and I did them without protest. I agree that chore's are good for one's character, but she assigned me the most treacherous of jobs as if she was doing her best to break me. I was already so broken. Living with her and dad in the home my mother had purchased felt like such a betrayal. One of my chores was to clean out and scrub the gutters along the sides of the house until they were gleaming white. If there was one speck of dirty rainwater, I would be punished to clean it again. Once, she sent me out to scrub the gutters in a terrible storm. I was outside on my knees, soaking wet, scrubbing, and scrubbing, almost mechanically. I looked up to see the gate to the yard opening and dad's car coming up the driveway. He spotted me out in the rain, rushed from the car, and took me into the house to confront my stepmom.

"What is this?" he asked angrily. "Why is Michelle out in the rain? Why is she scrubbing the gutters?" My stepmom stood speechless. Dad cursed at her and pushed her. He put me in the car and yelled at her to be out of the house by the time he got back. He drove me straight to the police station to file a report of child abuse. I sat there, having to describe all that had happened, and they took pictures of my bruised knees.

The marriage only lasted six months; this woman my father left my mother after seventeen years of marriage.

When we left the police station, dad took me back to my aunt's house and left me there with no explanation. I was so hurt and confused. I felt I must be bad luck; everyone I loved seemed to leave without explaining why. Even dad's family members were frustrated by him leaving me so abruptly. They would remark with distaste that dad had abandoned me. Over a month passed with no word from him. I had started to worry; my desire for acceptance and attention, combined with my fear of rejection and uncertainty.

This was the same auntie my sister was living with, and as they had kids of their own, space and money were very tight. Because my sister had a boyfriend at the time, she was barely around, so I suppose she was less of a burden than me. My granny who lived with my aunt, knew I could not stay there for long, so she started calling family and friends to ask if they could please take me until she could find a permanent place for me.

My granny was good to me. She had a way of making me feel better and helped teach me things a daughter usually learns from her mother. The day my stepmom sent me out of her sight and called me filthy, granny gave me the epaulettes from my mother's nursing uniform. I treasured them, these strips of cloth that my mother wore with such dignity. In my darkest times, these epaulettes would give me hope and comfort.

Granny would cook our leftover scraps to feed Jock and Tiffany, who were living by themselves at the now abandoned house in Phoenix. Every day, my cousin and I would walk to the old house, an hour there and an hour back, with big pots in our hands. We would feed the dogs and replenish their water. On one trip, we arrived to find Tiffany dead. Her body was caught in the yard gate, and I had to push hard to open it. Jock was sitting in the furthest corner, cowering timidly.

Anger arose in me. How could my father just leave my dogs there to die? The dogs had done nothing wrong. Why should they suffer? In truth, I was in pain because he had not been there to care for my mother, or for me. My perception of the mistreatment I had experienced was cloudy. I could see the abuse of my dogs better than I could see my own.

It was arranged for Jock to be given away because granny knew I couldn't continue to walk that far to care for him every day, and he couldn't survive on his own. The family that came for him seemed nice, but they had trouble getting him in the car. They came and picked me up so I could help them. Jock got in the car for me, and the family drove me back to my aunt's house. As they pulled away, I watched Jock scratch at the window trying to get back to me. My heart fell to the floor, seeing my best friend drive away. My dogs were the last remembrance of my happier times and my family before everything fell apart. Now, they too were gone.

It seemed that I was unwanted everywhere I went, and I could see granny's worry increase that I was not receiving the care I needed. She concluded that an orphanage was the only option for me. Being a developing country, South Africa has a long list of children waiting to get into orphanages. Before our initial appointment with child welfare came up, my aunt's family felt they could no longer keep me. Granny went around the neighborhood asking if anyone could take me in. A family who lived across the road agreed to help, and I lived with these kind strangers for about two weeks before they, too, grew tired of me.

Back at my aunt's house, granny's concern for me was increasing. I'd felt bad for causing so much worry, believing I was a burden to everyone. When our appointment came up, granny and I took a taxi to Phoenix Child Welfare. I remember granny speaking to the woman at child welfare saying, "Please look for a good Christian orphanage for her."

Soon after, granny received a call from one of her other daughters. She told her, "I will not let Gonum's daughter go to an orphanage!" she agreed to take me in. Dad's sisters had been close to my mother, and they looked up to her as an educated woman. I remember the look of relief on my granny's face, and her beautiful smile when she told me I would be going to live with my auntie's family in Pretoria, which was about 600 kilometers away.

I was happy that someone wanted me, and I thought I finally had a place to call "home" again. My aunt came to pick me up, and I said goodbye to my granny, sister, and childhood in Durban. As the car pulled away, I reflected on all I was leaving behind. I had lost so much. Now, the family I once knew was just a bittersweet memory.

"In the driest land you are not lost. God's mercy sees you."
- Michelle Felix

9

SEARCHING FOR BELONGING

I was eleven years old when I arrived in Pretoria to live with my auntie's family. I was grateful, and still am, that they gave me shelter, food, and education. They were the only ones to take me in and keep me from being placed in an orphanage. They had two small children, and both worked long days to provide for the family. Whatever chores they'd asked me to do, I would do. I felt it was the only way I could thank them.

One of my responsibilities before was to get up before school and put the laundry out to dry on the outside line. Then, I would clean the yard with a strong disinfectant called Jeyes Fluid, which was for cleaning and to stop unwanted creatures from entering the yard. Jeyes Fluid had a strong and distinct smell that would linger on my skin. At school, I tried to make friends, but the kids would laugh and tease me because I always reeked of it.

I would go home and try to scrub the smell from my skin. I hated this smell and that it created a new reason for me to be bullied at my new school. I was ashamed, and I did not know how to tell my aunt. To me, Jeyes Fluid smelled like rejection all over again.

Living with my auntie's family reminded me of all that I had lost. I remember watching them – my aunt, uncle, and their two kids – cuddling together on the couch watching television and aching for my own family, longing so much to belong to someone.

Perhaps I had too much time with my thoughts, but I could not stop myself from speculating that if only I had stayed with my mother when she begged me not to go to the wedding, she would still be here, and I would still have a mother. If only I had stayed, I could have saved my family. If only I had stayed, life would be different. These speculations played games with my mind and made me feel responsible for mum's death. Why was it that mum had helped bring life into the world almost every day, and yet she could not get the help she needed to save her own? These thoughts fed my guilt, and shame festered in me.

I was approaching my teen years, but I had no purpose or drive. I was just going through the motions of chores and school. I tried to focus on my studies in the hopes that I could make something of my life. Often, I would hide away in the library to study, but mostly it was to avoid my classmates. I was so fearful of being asked questions about my parents. How would I tell them that I lived with my aunt because my mother killed herself and my dad abandoned me? I hid myself, my past, and my pain. I thought covering it all up was my only chance at being accepted, and I was so desperate to belong.

Looking back on these moments, I needed to let go of the guilt and shame of not staying with mum. I could not control my mum's decision on July 17th. It was her choice and hers alone, and if I had stayed, could I have gone with her that night? We so often live life thinking everything could have been better if we did something else. I have learned to let go of things I could not control. I found healing by letting go of "If only I had stayed." Living in the present, and not the past, created new doors of healing for me.

"Every moment you live in the past is a moment you waste in the present."

\- Tony Robbins

10

SEEN & KNOWN

My aunt's family went to church regularly, and I looked forward to weekly services. The people at the church were welcoming and kind. Though I called upon God's name many times, I didn't really know who God was. I could not fully comprehend a true connection to someone unseen.

I was about thirteen years old when my understanding of God changed completely. We went to a mid-week service, called a "soaking meeting," at a church in Pretoria. There was no structure or formal service. People from all walks of life would come with their mats or towels and pray, worship, or read the Bible; but some would just sit. I was confused by it because the environment was so unlike anything I had seen before, people just sitting in stillness.

I lay on the floor, unsure what to do or expect. My thoughts quickly went from mum, then to dad, and then to everything that had happened in my young life. It felt like not only was I talking to God, but that He was listening.

I felt God tell me, "I see you; I know you, and I understand your pain."

I suddenly burst into tears, and I could not stop them from pouring out. Every emotion I had held back and hidden since mum had died was overflowing from within me. I felt God was grieving with me, that His tears were mixing with mine. I slowly felt an enormous weight being lifted from me. I knew something in me had shifted.

A young pastor came over to me and gently put his hand on my shoulder, asking if he could pray for me. This was the first time anyone had offered to pray for me, and I felt surrounded by love. I was aware that God had always been there. He answered my prayers when I called out to Him as I lay on the floor stricken by asthma, and in dozens of other moments when I needed protection and provision. He was always there, and it was in the stillness that I'd found Him.

We find God in different ways, and for me, this was the moment I had experienced God's heart as He wept with me in my pain. It was then that I gave my heart to God. This was the beginning of hope and healing.

After mum died, I lived in the shadows of others. Facing loss and rejection made me believe I had no purpose. I never knew who I was without my parents. I remember looking at myself in the mirror, not knowing why I even existed. For most of my childhood, I walked with my head lowered, feeling shame, hurt, and anger for the broken pieces in my life that I could not face or fix.

After this day, I no longer saw myself as merely taking up space. I knew I had a future, and a reason to live, and that the closer I came to God, the more I would understand my purpose. I'd realized my identity was not found in my parents nor the events that unfolded. My identity was found in my Maker, a higher power that created me. The hurdles in my life had brought me to this point of knowing God, which is the greatest gift I know. In my darkest moments, I was never alone-He was always there. I am my own person, and only I can walk my journey, which was created and uniquely crafted by the hands of God.

I started getting involved in the community and church, helping in Sunday School, outreach projects, and singing with the worship team. On Sundays, I never wanted to leave the church because there was so much love there. They knew my story and accepted and loved me all the same.

I became friends with the pastor's three daughters who grew to be like sisters to me. We did a lot of outreach work together in underprivileged settlements to support families. It felt good to help others in need because I understood how it feels to be vulnerable and confused as a child. On one mission trip, I talked to the kids about protecting themselves. I told them, "You have a right to refuse any kind of touch." A young girl burst into tears. My aunt and the pastor came and cared for her. We learned later that she was being molested at home, which shook me to my core.

I felt so angry at her mistreatment, so confused. I could not believe there were such horrible people in the world. I could feel the brokenness within her, but yet I was grateful that as a result of that moment of crying out, she would get the help she needed, that she would be protected. A few years later, I saw this young lady with a group of friends, and she was laughing and happy. It felt so good to see her smile.

Looking back on this moment, I've realized many of us hide our pain so deep inside we sometimes forget it is there until it surfaces beyond our control. For the longest time, I hid all my emotions and feelings, always afraid to talk about mum's death. It was uncomfortable, especially when depression was not considered a real illness, and suicide was looked at as an act of cowardness.

After my second year in school, I made two friends, Bianca and Itumeleng. When I told them about my parents, they did not judge me, and it felt good to be truly known and accepted all the same. Itumeleng and I would walk home from school and talk about all the things we wanted to do in life. They were far-fetched dreams for girls in our circumstances, but we believed they were possible. I wanted to be educated like my mother and go to college. I had hoped to be a nurse and work at the same hospital that she did. I dreamt of being self-sufficient, not dependent on anyone for help or happiness.

Bianca had the most beautiful singing voice and talked about becoming a famous singer like Whitney Houston. She had a hard life too, and I could tell her anything without feeling ashamed. She would sing all the time, and my favorite was "His Eye Is on the Sparrow."

I sing because I'm happy
I sing because I'm free
For His eye is on the sparrow,
And I know He watches over me.

\- Civilla Martin

11

APARTMENT 27

ranny continued to search for my father, (her son). She called my aunt's house one day, and I was overjoyed to speak with her; I missed her so much. After asking how I was doing, and how school was going, she told me that she thought she had located my dad. It appeared he was living back in Durban, and she even had an address. Relief and hope arose in my heart after hearing he was okay. This was such great news! He did not know where I was living, and I was certain he was looking for me, too.

I developed a plan to go to him. Every Friday, my aunt and uncle gave me R5 to purchase a school lunch instead of bringing a homemade lunch. Every Friday, I saved the money and went without lunch. I remember the hunger, watching the other students enjoying their hamburgers and chips, but I was determined to get to my father.

For three months I secretly saved my Friday lunch money until I had enough to purchase a bus ticket to Durban. It was mid-way through the school year, and when my aunt and granny learned of my plan, they forbade me to go. But now that I knew where to find Dad, nothing could stop me from getting to him. At thirteen years old, I climbed on a Greyhound bus to Durban. The nine-hour journey gave me plenty of time to dream of our reunion. Dad and I would be a family again, and the whole world would know he did not abandon me after all.

At the bus station in Durban, I somehow negotiated a ride in a taxi bus to the address my granny had told me. I reached the apartment building and climbed to the third floor. Standing in front of the door, I looked back at the paper to verify the address. Apartment 27. I heard my father's voice on the other side of the door, providing further confirmation that I had found him. I knocked hopefully, eager to see his face and fall into his embrace. The door opened, and I was face to face with my father for the first time in three years. The smile on my face exposed my excitement and joy, but his face was blank.

"What are you doing here?" he said.

In the background, I heard a woman asking who was at the door. "It's just someone selling something," he called back to her. "Nothing to worry about."

He turned back to me, and in a hushed voice told me to wait downstairs before shutting the door in my face. I was stunned. This certainly was not the reunion I expected or that my heart so longed to have. I had been so confident that my father would be ecstatic to see me. I did as I was instructed and went downstairs, waiting for quite some time in the heat with my heavy bag. Finally, dad came and told me to get in the car. He drove me to the home of an older couple, gave them a little money, and left me there. He did not say much to me. It seemed like he was still in shock to see me.

For the first couple of weeks, I was there, I assumed dad was working on finding a place for us to be together and be a family. At the house where he left me, the man would go to work every day, so the woman and I would spend the days together. She had some special needs and could not communicate well, but we enjoyed each other's company. She made the best tea, and we would sit together, cook together, and sometimes go for walks. When the man would come home, he would drink heavily and get angry, and the environment would change. It frightened me, and I started staying in my room when he came home. I was grateful to have a place to go although there wasn't much to my room. There was no bed; the couple just put a sheet on the floor, and that is where I slept. They did what they could.

Dad would come to visit once or twice a week, but he spent more time talking to the man than he did to me. He never seemed happy to see me and was more stressed about what he was going to do with me. He would drop off money to the man to help with my care. After about two months, the man told my dad I could no longer live there. He said to my father that it wasn't proper for me to be sleeping on the floor, and that I needed to be in school. "How long are you going to hide her?" the man had asked him.

I couldn't understand why dad had stashed me here to live in the shadows with strangers. Now I know that the woman who had asked who was at the door was his new wife, and she didn't know that he had children. I had longed to find my dad and wanted to believe that he wanted to be with me, too. Decades later, I would learn that he had created a whole new identity for himself, even going so far as to change his hair and create an identification card that said he was ten years younger than he actually was.

When it was obvious, I could no longer stay with the couple, dad told me I had to go back to Pretoria. I asked him why, but he wouldn't give me a straight answer. On the long bus ride to Pretoria, I again sunk into a low place. I had made the trip to find him with such hope in my heart, only to be rejected again. I searched for a reason, to understand what I had done wrong for dad not to want me. I was so certain that this plan to find him, would redeem all the brokenness and rejection. I was absolutely devastated. For the first time, I accepted that the one person I believed would still want me, did not. I was utterly alone.

"What feels like rejection is often God's protection
when you're heading in the wrong direction."
- Donna Partow

12

BROKEN & ASHAMED

My return to Pretoria was soaked in shame. When I walked into my aunt's house, everyone was silent. Their quiet stares screamed at me, "We told you so." Through the lens of my broken heart, everyone, and everything around me said that I was unwanted.

I had missed too much school to return to my class, and thus I had to repeat the whole of grade eight. This gave my classmates a new reason to bully me, taunting me that I had to repeat the grade because I was stupid. Even more anger and frustration arose in me. I had wasted a year of my life trying to find my father, only to have him reject me once again. I seemed to have nothing that people wanted. I walked with my head down, and I didn't speak unless someone spoke to me, which no one did. Who would want anything to do with such a broken girl?

The church was different. There I could open up, and I felt loved and accepted. Still, this new cycle of rejection had dragged me down into darkness again. I had regretted going to find my father. Perhaps not knowing would have been better than having him discard me again.

More darkness seemed to want to overwhelm me, but now I knew to call upon God. I prayed that God would send something or someone to give me hope. I prayed God would heal my heart again. There were so many dreams I had for my future that once again seemed out of reach. When the darkness would creep in, I would pray for a sign or any reason to believe that there was something good in store for my future. Slowly, I again found my peace in God, and hope returned.

Not long after my return, my sister found her way to Pretoria. I was so happy to have a piece of my family back with me. I had not seen or spoken to her since I had left Durban following the incident with my stepmother. During that time, my sister had experienced her own trials, falling pregnant at sixteen, attempting a marriage that didn't last, and leaving her child and ex-husband.

She was eager for a new start, and my aunt let her stay with us while she looked for a job and got back on her feet. It had been our mother's last wish that we would stay together, and my sister felt compelled to honor that wish. And she, too, was seeking healing. She hoped that reunification with me not only would make mum proud, but also would help to redeem some of our mutual brokenness. As for me, I hoped this was our chance to finally have a relationship. I longed to know my sister and create new family memories together in honor of our mum.

My uncle helped my sister secure a job where he was working, and after about two months, she was ready to move into her own place and wanted me to join her. It was an easy "yes," for me but my aunt and uncle wanted me to stay with them until I finished school. Though they protested, ultimately, they let me go, I think because they knew of my mother's last wish for us to be together.

"We are powerful and perfectly created. Dare to dream, my beautiful sisters."

- Michelle Felix

Memories with my sister.

13

MUM'S LAST WISH

I was sixteen when I moved in with my sister. It was a small accommodation called an "out-building" and typically, the main home attached to it was where the landlords lived. We didn't have much, but my sister's job provided for our rent and a little food. This was enough for me; I was thrilled just to be with my sister.

I was in a new school now, as my aunt had transferred me after the bullying for repeating a grade, and my school was just two blocks from our little place. I made three good friends there, and we called ourselves "The Four Musketeers." None of us had money to do the things teenagers normally do, like go to movies or parties, so after school, and on the weekends, we spent most of our time together just talking, listening to music, and enjoying each other's company.

In my last year of high school, I had met my first boyfriend. He was quite a bit older, and when he first began to pursue me, I thought he must be playing a game. He was very popular and had previously dated very beautiful girls.

He complimented me all the time, telling me I was beautiful, which was not something I had ever been told. He brought me roses and chocolates and took me clothes shopping because I didn't have much clothing. He absolutely spoiled me with everything a teenage girl could want. It was the first time in my life that a male had paid attention to me.

I had always envied the pretty girls at school. Now, more than ever, I wanted to look like them so that he would stay with me. I started to have even more insecurities about my appearance. I did not like my short hair, and my weight had always been a struggle for me, particularly after turning to food for comfort after mum's death. Now that I had a boyfriend, I was determined to lose weight. I found myself feeling guilty when I would eat or even think about eating, so afraid that he would leave me.

About six months into dating, he changed seemingly overnight. His caring and, attentive ways turned verbally, emotionally, and even physically abusive. I remember the first time he pushed and slapped me. I was stunned, but I blamed myself, concluding that I must have done something to change his actions toward me so severely. Yet, he had been the first male to show affection toward me, and I could not imagine my life without him.

Despite the mistreatment, I genuinely hoped he would not leave me. There were more instances of physical abuse, and yet I would always go back to him, crying for his forgiveness. This is the cruel twist that abuse plays on a heart longing to be loved. I had not yet known a healthy kind of love, and I did not see at the time that this wasn't love at all. I was also scared that if he left me, no other man would ever want me.

During one of our break-ups. I was leaving my house to go visit church friends, and, as I was closing the gate, he was suddenly behind me. He screamed at me to get back in the house. In the past, I would have obeyed out of fear, but on this occasion, I felt courage. He was shocked that I was not backing down and gave one more order to get back in the house. I turned to walk away, and he grabbed me by the neck and threw me against a brick wall. My sister came running out of the house and confronted him. "Stop! You are going to kill my sister!" It was the first time I could recall my sister speaking up for me.

At that moment, I finally saw how toxic our relationship was. Nothing good could come from it, and I knew I had to end it. We broke up, and though my first heartbreak was hard, I truly believed better things were in store for me.

I quickly realized that I had been living my mother's life. I had been desperate to be with this man despite his abusive ways, just as my mother was desperate to stay with my dad even though he mistreated her. Mum didn't feel she could love anyone else, and probably that no one else could love her. Dad seemed to encourage that line of thinking. My mother was so beautiful and intelligent; I still cannot imagine anyone wanting anything but the best for her.

Looking back on this time, I know the importance of loving yourself first and truly knowing you are worthy of love before you let someone love you. We accept what we believe we deserve, and the brokenness in me had me convinced that I deserved very little. In time, I began to see that it wasn't love at all, because love is kind. I began to see myself the way God sees me and believed that I deserved a love that is kind and honoring.

About a year later, he called the house, and the sound of his voice still provoked fear in me. At first, he was silent and then he told me he was sorry for everything he had done to hurt me. He said that I had not deserved to be treated that way. Relief washed over me; it appeared that he was genuinely sorry. I said, "I forgive you," and that was it. That apology, that proper acknowledgment of responsibility for his actions, was the honor my soul knew I deserved, despite my brokenness insisting that I didn't.

When my sister lost her job, I started looking for work. We had no money for rent, and she was too ashamed to go to our aunt for help. For several weeks we ate only bread and black tea. Around this time, Granny came to Pretoria to visit my aunt, and she stopped in to see us. I was delighted to see her, but she was extremely distressed when she saw our living conditions and bare cupboards. She went next door to speak with the landlord who told her we hadn't paid our rent in four months, but she didn't have the heart to kick us out because she knew we had no money to pay. I will be eternally grateful for the mercy she showed us.

I had followed granny into the landlord's house and heard as granny asked to use her phone. She dialed, and after a moment, she spoke sternly, "Sunthuras, your children need you. It's time for you to step up and be a father. These girls have nothing." After an extended phone call and tongue lashing from his mother, I don't know what changed in my dad, but he agreed to tell his wife the truth about his daughters and past life.

"You deserve love that will make you believe in love."
- Unknown

14

HOPE BREAKS THROUGH

Dad paid for my bus ticket to Durban; my sister stayed behind, I'm not sure why. Although I wanted so much to see him, I could not shake the pain of rejection from the last time I had made this trip. I was fearful of meeting the woman who had called to him as I stood in the doorway of Apartment 27, the woman my father was afraid to tell that he had children.

The day he picked me up from the bus stop was September 11, 2001. News footage of the chaos at the World Trade Center in The United States was on the television as we came into the apartment. Here I was finally reunited with my father, and across the world, incalculable tragedy and loss were overwhelming a nation. Dad was understandably distracted by the world news, but I hoped he would show at least some interest in me.

I met my new stepmom, and she was nice enough. I imagine she was still processing the shock of learning that her husband had two daughters. She made attempts to get to know me, but she mainly seemed to be trying to sort out how drastically her life had suddenly changed.

A few weeks later, dad sent for my sister. There was no bedroom for us as my stepmother's brother lived with them as well, taking up the second bedroom. I had been sleeping on the floor in the lounge, and then my sister joined me there. It was uncomfortable, both due to the tight quarters and the adjustments all of us were navigating.

My dad was not as I remembered him from my childhood. He seemed to avoid my sister and me; perhaps it was out of fear as to how his wife might react if he showed affection toward us. Living there, we felt more like boarders than daughters living in their father's home. My sister and I were eager to find work, so we could move to our own place.

Dad's cousin owned a clinical laboratory. He got me my first job there as a courier, which was the best job they could offer me being that I was straight out of high school with no work experience. I would walk all over town in the rain, extreme heat, or whatever the day brought to deliver blood test results to doctors' offices. My earnings were just enough to pay my dad to board at his home, plus a little left over for food and bus money.

My sister got a job there too, and, since she had some work experience, they hired her for the insurance department. After six months, I was promoted to an administrative clerk. When we had saved enough, my sister and I got our own apartment one floor down from my father and stepmom, and it was good to have more breathing room from the tension, as well as more physical space for ourselves.

My dad and stepmom had found a church that they attended regularly and seemed to have established relationships and a sense of community there. Every Sunday we all went together, and I was so glad to be back in church. Dad hadn't told the pastors or church members about his former life, and so, instead of going to church as his daughters, my sister and I were known at the church as his nieces.

The pastors would talk to me about my "uncle," and I would play along, but it hurt my heart and my soul to participate in this lie. It was a new form of rejection and abandonment to be denied by my father in that way. My sister and I did not question it or attempt to bring the truth to light. As wonderful as it was to be back in church, the pretending was painful. After about six months, dad finally admitted that we were actually his daughters. I started to get involved in the youth ministry. I founded the El Shaddai creative arts school for young adults. These kids brought so much happiness and hope to my life. Together, we laughed, cried, danced, and encouraged each other. The friendships we made through music and dance still exists today.

Living with my sister again was good. We were slowly building a strong connection and were grateful that we had each other. But she met a man and quickly moved out, eager to get away from our dad and stepmom and the reminders of all the pain he had caused. Though dad had obviously been making attempts to repair his relationship with us, he never apologized for anything. My sister struggled to forgive him, and really, how could you blame her? She had her own pain, as well as her own healing to find. She had known our mother better, since she was five years older than me and had many more memories of our family than I did.

When my sister moved out, I tried my best to pay the rent on my own. However, despite working seven days a week, eventually, I had to move back in with my dad. I continued to work hard, hopeful that I could find my way out of this cycle. I desperately wanted to work toward the dreams that God had put on my heart to go to college and pursue an education as my mother did.

It turned out that several of the nurses at the lab where I was working had worked with my mother. When they realized I was her daughter, they gushed about how talented and admired she was. Hearing these things about my mother meant the world to me. For years, I had craved to hear anyone even mention her name. Their stories helped revive my memories as well as bolster my hope. One nurse, Maya, had even gone to school with mum, and she would brag to me about her skill and intelligence. This increased my longing to make something of my life, just as my mother had. Maya taught me how to draw blood and encouraged me to take a phlebotomy program through the company. I was accepted to the program and got another small promotion as a phlebotomist.

During this time, my father and stepmother were frequently fighting. She had a mood disorder, and whenever she and dad argued, she would take it out on me. I felt I was back at the house in Phoenix with my first stepmom. I knew I needed out of this environment and their cycle of hostility. I could not help but question God. It seemed that every time I found a bit of happiness, it never lasted long. I always end up feeling unwanted, and there seemed to be no way out. I did not have enough money to even get out of my father's house, much less to pursue my dream of attending college. Furthermore, dad did not have sufficient means to help me either. I prayed and prayed for God to give me a sign; and waited, but admittedly with waning hope.

One evening, while on a break at work, I picked up a newspaper and saw an article that said the United Kingdom was accepting applications from South Africans for a working-holiday visa. Amazingly, I met the minimum requirements: being at least eighteen years of age and having a high school diploma. I didn't have the money to leave South Africa, but I still applied and then waited for a miracle.

What I did not know at the time is that mum had put some money away for my sister and me to be made available to us when we turned a certain age. She made sure that only we could collect it, not my father or anyone else. Dad told me about the money, and, not long after, I received notification that I was granted the visa to the United Kingdom.

I was thrilled and determined to take this opportunity and money from mum and make a future for myself. This money, this manna from heaven, had come precisely at the right time. I knew this was an answer to my prayers, to my cries to God for help and a way out. I needed this opportunity to help me believe my dreams were possible. Dad was immensely proud of me and would tell everyone he saw about my upcoming travels. He had to know that I was not happy at home and that this was the chance at a hopeful future that he could never give me.

Dad and his brothers and sisters and their families came to see me off at the Johannesburg airport. At the gate, I looked back into the crowd of family members. I wanted a final glimpse of my dad before boarding, but I couldn't find him. My eyes scanned the airport lobby, and I found him tucked in a corner wiping his eyes with his handkerchief. It was the first time I had ever seen my father cry. It hit me squarely at that moment: my dad loves me.

My heart flooded with compassion for him and forgiveness immediately followed. Seeing his daughter go off with such hope of better things for me seemed to give him some relief from the shame he carried over my tumultuous childhood. He had let his daughters down so much over the years. He had never once told me that he loved me. Holding out for an apology from him or some indication that he loved me had made me bitter and resentful for many years. At that moment, I saw both his brokenness and his regret, and I knew with certainty that he loved me.

Choosing to forgive my father that day created such a powerful change in me. It felt like freedom, joy, and peace all at once. It felt as though God had given me a new heart, and the wounds I had carried over my father's abandonment were washed away.

Learning to forgive, rather than just hoping to forget, was one of the most challenging steps in my healing journey. It is easy to say the words, "I forgive you," but have you really forgiven? Washed away all records of wrong? After being reunited with dad back in Apartment 27 in Durban, I usually did not feel anger toward him. It seemed that life mostly carried on normally. But there were moments, like when the nurses spoke of my mum or I would recall the times my dad left me and rejected me, when resentment would boil up within me.

I had hoped to simply forget the past and that if I could do that, the resentment would fade. Holding on to anger made me a bitter person, and it was holding me back from finding peace. I was robbing myself of happiness. Carrying this burden of anger for my father was destroying me. However, I believed that if he would just humble himself, ask me to forgive him, and accept at least some responsibility for our broken lives, it would set me free. He never did, and ultimately, that was okay.

The day that I had left for the UK, I had accepted that my dad was only human. We all make mistakes, and though his mistakes had caused me deep suffering, I somehow knew in that moment at the airport that he was doing all he was capable of, and I saw and felt his love for me. No longer did I need my father to seek my forgiveness. That day, God showed me my fathers' heart, and my soul was at peace.

"Forgiveness liberates the soul. It removes fear. That is why it is such a powerful weapon."

\- Nelson Mandela

15

PREPARE FOR TAKE OFF

As I buckled into my seat preparing for my very first airplane ride, it finally sunk in that I was leaving my homeland for a new continent. I had made virtually no plans for myself in London, although to give my family comfort, I lied and told them I had a job and a place to stay. The latter at least was true; I had a flat share arranged, and the money from my mother would cover my part of the rent for one month. As the wheels lifted from the ground, I put my head in my hands and thought, "Michelle what have you done?" I was already on my way and removing the safety net of family and familiarity was exactly what I needed to take this bold step toward my dreams.

I landed at Heathrow, cleared customs, and set out to find the tube to my accommodation. I went in the wrong direction three times before I found the London Underground station, only to get on the wrong train. I went in a circle again before finally, asking for help. My initial lessons for living abroad: always read the signs,

make sure you can read a map, and never be ashamed to
ask for help!

Arriving in London was invigorating. I was so eager for
a change and a chance to build a future. I had been moved
around so much, but this time, the move was my choice, and
God had orchestrated every detail to make it possible. All
my life I had been so fragile and prone to fear; the asthmatic
girl who blended into the background. God had changed
me; when I listened to Him, He made me brave. This was a
new and courageous Michelle, in a new city, with a visa, and
just enough money for one month of rent.

My priority was to find a job. Every day, I was out from
morning until evening looking about town for work. I was
open to anything, but each day ended with my tube card
at its daily max and no job. With money dwindling, I went
a whole week eating only beans and toast. After paying the
agency for the last week of rent I could afford, I dropped
to my knees and prayed, "Lord, I don't want to be a failure.
I don't want to go back and have to tell my family that I
couldn't make it on my own.

It may seem like a vain prayer, and certainly there is
nothing wrong with failure. But I needed to believe that
my life could turn in a new direction. It is said that faith
the size of a mustard seed can move a mountain, this is true
of what happened next. After a month of searching for
work with no success, I suddenly got a job offer working at
a call center.

I was so incredibly grateful for the job, for any job. However, working in a call center was highly incompatible for me because I had so much apprehension about talking to strangers. The manager tracked our call logs to see how many calls we were making per day. So, I would dial, and then set the phone down on the desk without saying a word. One day, my supervisor came to me and said, "Michelle, how is it that you make nearly five hundred calls each day, but you have no sales?" Of course, I knew the reason-it is hard to close a sale when you're too nervous to even talk to the customer! We both knew this was not the job for me.

Fortunately, God provided another job for me as a live-in caregiver which also meant I would no longer need to pay rent. I earned enough that I could even send money home to my dad and stepmom who were both out of work. Every two weeks or, so I was given a new assignment in a new location. My job took me all over the U.K. from the countryside to the city, from Buckinghamshire to Windsor. I lived in people's homes and cared for their elderly, vulnerable, or physically or mentally challenged loved ones. My clients came from all walks of life, and I thoroughly enjoyed caring for them.

At one point, I was assigned to a job for Cecil Edward Guinness, a descendant of the esteemed brewing family at his home in a small town in the country. His wife had an injury from a fall, and I cared for her for approximately three months through her recovery. They were wonderful people. I would wake up at six a.m. and take a scenic walk in the beautiful countryside. It was the most beautiful place, lush and green with the sounds of birds chirping, which started my mornings in a place of serenity. At night, we would talk over dinner and then watch documentaries on the Discovery Channel together.

Every Sunday, I went to church with Mr. and Mrs. Guinness. It was a traditional church with wooden benches and the playing of hymns. It was my first time in a traditional church compared to growing up in a Baptist church with boisterous clapping of hands, drums, and casual entire. I was nervous about my first visit to their church, but everyone made me feel welcomed and loved.

Mr. and Mrs. Guinness left such a special place in my heart, especially watching their love for each other. Mr. Guinness cared for Mrs. Guinness with patience, compassion, and respect. It was so beautiful to see the love between a husband and wife in its purest form. It gave me hope to find true love one day. When that job concluded, Mr. Guinness wrote me a lovely reference by hand in the most elegant cursive. I still have it and will always treasure it.

I had another assignment at a facility for individuals with disabilities in Aylesbury, in central England. The assignment was for six weeks, and I did not want it to end when it was over. The facility housed a community of people with various disabilities living their best lives. There was such joy in this place! I was assigned to care for a 42-year-old man who was paralyzed from the waist down due to polio. I would take him to his medical appointments and to the social gatherings hosted by the facility.

I absolutely loved the social gatherings. Most were organized to promote positive living for people with disabilities, and it was inspiring to see their resilience, creativity, and positivity. We went to the movies and went on lunch outings. When we were out, some people would stare at us, especially when entering the cinema or restaurant with twenty wheelchairs, but it did not discourage my client or the other residents. They were happy to be alive and found joy in making memories together.

To me, it was an honor to be in their presence and observe their joyful approach to life. I admired their courage to withstand discrimination and adversity, and that their hearts remained unaffected and still full of love. My friends in Aylesbury left lifelong footprints in my heart and taught me that making excuses for the setbacks and tragedies in our lives will only hold us back. They showed me that determination gives you wings to soar. Spending those six weeks with them instilled in me a lasting gratitude for life and all it brings.

My time of independence in the U.K. held so much joy. I made wonderful friends and was able to serve at Hillsong Church in London. When I was in-between assignments, I had to find a place to live, and I would always seek out the cheapest possible rental. On one occasion, I got completely lost looking for my accommodation. As it grew darker and the air colder, I knew I had to find my way or sleep outside. I remember telling myself, that you will be strong when being strong is the only choice you have. It was a moment that further persuaded me that I was indeed strong, and that my life would not take the course that my mother's life did. I kept searching, and a kind man helped me with directions. I had walked past the place three times because the entrance was hidden between shops. After I settled and was lying down on the bed, I cried with so much gratitude to have shelter over my head.

Sometimes, during my time off from work, I would stay with my South African friends I had met while staying in my first accommodation. They were like sisters to me. We traveled to Wales, Scotland, Ireland, and Europe together. We had all come from humble beginnings and were so excited to seize this amazing opportunity to live and work in a first world country. We made incredible memories and lifelong friendships.

On Sundays, I was at church from seven in the morning until five in the evening serving on the host team. I would help tidy up and set up the church with reading materials and then welcome everyone to church for the afternoon service. After serving, we would have group lunches in the city of Tottenham. I also made memorable friendships here through coming together to serve the community.

The teaching centered around the belief that the church is loving God, and loving God is to love people, no matter how broken or lost. I felt that love and acceptance every time I walked through the doors, and the love of God became more real for me than ever before. I would end the day on Sundays by joining the evening service to strengthen my relationship with God. It was my time with God, and I had never known a peace so real until I found Him.

One evening, I was riding the tube, listening to the hymn, "It Is Well with My Soul." I had heard it many times before, but this evening it brought up an unexpected emotion in me. It became a prayer to God, a declaration of letting go of past confusion. I had been infected with anger toward my mother for leaving me and haunted by the questions: "What if I had stayed?" Could I have saved her?

It is well.
    With my soul.
        It is well...it is well... with my soul.

As the lyrics washed over me, it was as if the shame, anger, and guilt fell from me and onto the floor of the train. My tears that night was tears of agreement with God; indeed, it was well with my soul.

I learned to embrace my imperfections and truly see my self-worth. I came to the U.K. with the hope that God had a purpose for me. My time in the U.K. cemented that hope into a strong faith. I could see God's hand and protection throughout my life. He had never left me, and I knew

He would see me through anything that was to come. My response to Him was a posture of surrender: I will walk through the fire with you, knowing you are with me.

As my time in the U.K came to an end, I wanted to stay but was unable to extend my visa. There was a teary goodbye with my friends, and I was headed back to South Africa, and to move back in with my dad and stepmom. My stepmother's perception of me had seemed to change; she was more accepting of me. I knew that I had changed. I no longer searched for my worth in my dad or my lost mother or anything or anyone. My worth was in God.

Living in the U.K. had shown me that I could thrive even when stepping into the unknown on my own. Yes, there were moments of loneliness, doubt, and fear, but it was during these moments that I had discovered strengths I never knew were in me. Stepping out of my comfort zone created a new world of possibilities. My time in the U.K. had secured lifelong friendships, teachable moments, a new career path, a deeper relationship with God, and a new understanding of myself.

"Let your setbacks fuel your desire to succeed."
                                                    - Michelle Felix

16

THE CHILDREN OF UMTATA

After six months of living back in Durban, the tension between dad and my stepmom continued to escalate. Sometimes they fought late into the night, and one night the argument got physical. They both were throwing things around the house, and my stepmom was screaming to try and wake up the neighbors. It was awful. Dad's anger was clearly increasing, and after the fight, my stepmom would lock herself in the bedroom for days. My dad had developed diabetes, and it would flare up and make him ill. It felt like I was reliving my childhood, and my mind went back to the arguments at home before mum and dad separated.

It felt unnatural to be back in that volatile state. The old circumstances I'd faced growing up in South Africa didn't match with who God had made me to be during my time in the U.K. My growing relationship with my father was the only thing that felt congruent to the new me. We would play pool together, watch war movies, and have long conversations. During one talk, he admitted to me that he would never find a woman like my mother. It was the first time I've ever heard him express any kind of regret, and the closest he would come to apologizing for his part in my mom's despair or what he had put my sister and I through. It was enough for me because I knew that forgiveness was mine to offer, and I had already given it that day at the airport. I saw no need to hold onto my anger.

I was able to come back to my phlebotomist job, but before I started, I wanted to find a way to serve as a form of thanks for all that God had done in my life. I signed up for a mission trip with the Africa International Volunteer Group to teach in rural and impoverished areas of Africa. I was the only one in the group that was from Africa, the rest had come from the United States, Europe, and other first-world nations.

I taught English to the village children under a tree and creative arts in an orphanage. We also helped the villagers learn to plant vegetables. There were few resources, no paper or pencils, and most of the children didn't have shoes. While this simplicity resonated with me, I marveled at the children's uncommon joy. Joy was not something I saw or felt in my childhood.

We eventually got use of a blackboard, and one day I was teaching but getting increasingly frustrated because many of the children were not paying attention. They seemed to be intentionally turning away from me. My co-teacher, who was standing behind the children, also noticed this, and told me he thought he knew what the problem was. He contacted a friend who was an optometrist and asked him if he would be willing to come and examine the children. We learned that almost seventy percent of the children had impaired vision due to malnutrition. It wasn't that they weren't interested in the lesson; they simply could not see it. I imagine it must have been so frustrating to those children for me to insist on pointing to words on a blackboard that they could not see.

So often we look at circumstances and draw conclusions before we seek a deeper understanding. My wise colleague sought understanding, and as a result, the children in need of eyeglasses in an entire village were equipped with them, thanks to generous sponsors who funded them. The glasses made a world of difference for the children. They were eager to learn and seeing their happy, bespectacled faces is a treasured memory.

Once while on a hike, we saw a group of children- with bare and swollen feet walking and carrying water buckets on their shoulders. They had been walking for hours to get water home to their families, which they often did daily. They were weary but still smiling. One little boy was very small, probably only four or five years old. I stopped near him and went to my knees. He came into my arms and fell asleep almost immediately. It was as if he just needed a moment, a place of safety, and the warmth of a gentle touch. He had needed a hug as much as he needed water to drink.

When we stretch out our hands to help others, it helps us to see life through grateful eyes. I had known hardship just as these sweet children did. I had been deeply affected by the loss of my mum, but these children were facing the brutalities of life with virtually no help at all. I found even more healing through my time with the children of Umtata. The children had so little, yet they lived life with big smiles, optimism, and hope. Talking with them, and sharing stories of hope, increased my own hope and happiness. They had dreams, and aspirations even though their circumstances were appalling, and it was my great privilege to encourage them to believe in their dreams.

I shared with them my perspective of the rainbow, which was quite different from others. Many people see the rainbow as joyful or a new beginning, which is true, but I also saw the rainbow's colors as a sign that not every day will be blue skies. There will be good days and bad days, but there is always hope in even the bleakest of places.

My time with the Africa International Volunteer Group showed me that helping others can help heal our own brokenness. We often let our pain turn into bitterness, but these children took their pain and hardship and used it as inspiration for their dreams.

I have always been a believer in planting seeds and watching others grow from those seeds. There are seasons in our life that are specifically meant for sowing seeds, making a difference, and hoping the seeds we planted will blossom into something that would inspire others.

Being grateful for the smallest things in life can open doors to healing. I found healing knowing I was helping others and making a difference in my community. I certainly did not have the power to change every child's circumstance, but I hoped that the time spent with them brought purpose and encouragement: to believe in themselves and not the circumstances that surround them. The children of Umtata hold a permanent place in my heart. I was truly blessed to know them.

"A belief that we are defined by our compassion and kindness toward others."

- Ubuntu

An Unforgettable Journey

17

FEELING HER EMBRACE

I focused on my phlebotomy job, hoping to save any bit of money left over from helping my dad and stepmom, still hopeful for an opportunity to get an education. One day, two women came into the clinic who appeared to be related-possibly sisters- and although I could not place either of them, they somehow seemed familiar to me. One was our patient, and after she got signed in for her blood draw, the other woman went to wait in the car. I could not stop glancing at the woman who remained inside, certain that she was, or at least resembled, someone I once knew. When the clerk handed me her intake forms, and I read her name, my breath stopped: Mandy. I remembered playing on mum's sister's farm with my cousins: Mandy, Martha, and Mervin.

My hands shook as I wrapped the tourniquet around her arm. I looked at the woman and asked, "Is your mum Panjalay?"

Mandy studied my face, taking in my features, and suddenly gasped, "Kabashini?" My sister's name.

"No," I answered. "It's Michelle."

She burst into tears and ran to the car yelling for Martha to come. We embraced and sobbed together. They told me the family had been looking for me everywhere. I had not seen my mother's family since the day of her burial when I was eleven years old, but I had always hoped I would find them again. I never imagined they would be looking for me.

All my childhood memories at the farm in Glendale came flooding back to me. These were the happiest times with my family. Mum was always carefree and at ease there, and seeing my cousins was like seeing my happy mum once again. I smiled to myself as I recalled things like eating chicken curry on a banana leaf and laying on the green grass watching the stars with my family.

We exchanged numbers and, later that week, Mandy took me to her house for an amazing feast. I met mum's beautiful sisters. I felt honored to be in their presence and saw my mum's smile in both of them.

The chicken curry tasted just as I remembered it, and my aunties seemed not to have aged. They showered me with love, and my auntie even sneaked money into my purse, following the Indian tradition of the eldest treating the youngest with a money gift. While we were together, Mandy devised a plan to surprise the rest of the family by bringing me to her upcoming wedding.

Telling dad that I had reunited with mum's family was difficult. I was scared at first, but he did not say much or show any emotions. He knew I then began visiting mum's family often; however, he did not ask me about my visits with them. Perhaps it brought back memories of mum, or maybe it reminded him of all his regrets.

Every time I would visit mum's sisters in Stanger Durban, I've felt mum's warm embrace again. My aunties shared stories with me about her, and they always made me smile. Knowing more about mum made me feel closer to her. When my aunt first saw me, tears welled in her eyes. She told me I looked identical to mum, and that seeing me made her feel like mum was there again.

My dad's sister accompanied me to Mandy's wedding. She got me a beautiful blue saree and helped me dress. She knew it was a big day for me, being reunited with mum's whole family after many years. My emotions fluctuated between nervousness and excitement; it truly was like meeting them for the first time since so many years had passed. I was most excited to see mum's brother.

Mum had adored her brother, and they were extremely close. At the wedding, my aunt helped point him out to me. I was nervous and did not want to approach him alone, so she took me over to him. Walking toward my uncle and aunt, not knowing what to say, my heart raced, and my hands shook.

My uncle was sitting with his wife, and they clearly did not recognize me. My auntie reintroduced me, "This is Gonum's daughter, your niece-Michelle." Once again, I was enveloped in tear-soaked embraces by the family that loved me and wanted to know me. I had lived for years with only a few memories of my mother, and no one around to help keep her memory alive. Reuniting with mum's family, hearing her name over and over, and learning more about what she was like brought me closer to her. I had always desperately hoped to make a connection with them and had intended to go in search for them as soon as I got a car.

I know with certainty that a "higher power" arranged for Mandy and me to be reunited that day at the lab. There were other labs they could have gone to in the city, but she ended up in my lab and as my patient. I wasn't even supposed to be working that day. It was my day off, but I picked up a shift to earn some extra money. It was always mum's desire that I would stay connected to her family, and I feel she helped make this seemingly chance meeting happen, reuniting me with these dear loved ones. Some may call it a coincidence, but I call it God's perfect plan.

"Coincidence is God's way of remaining anonymous."
- Albert Einstein

18

MY AMERICAN DREAM

Practically overnight, I had a community of family around me to share in my life. I told my cousins of my dream to get an education and become a nurse like my mother. Two of my cousins had already applied for the green card lottery in the hopes of coming to America, and they suggested that I apply, too. The application process was expensive, and I had very little savings left. Almost all of the earnings from my job went to pay for rent and basic needs since dad was still out of work.

Yet I felt this could be my last chance to leave South Africa, to make something of my life. The green card application would be valid for nine years, and I resolved that even if it took nine years for me to get to America, I had to try. I submitted my application in June, and a few months later I received a call notifying me that I had been selected for a green card. Only nine applicants were selected from South Africa. The woman on the phone told me the next steps would be difficult, and she was right. It took me eight months to complete the necessary paperwork.

The final step of the process was to go to Johannesburg for an in-person interview. I was so nervous knowing that all these months of effort and my last bit of savings could be all for nothing if the interview did not go well. My cousin graciously drove me to the appointment and gave me his best wishes. After a long day, at the US embassy, going through the different stages of the interview, the decision came.

I remember the moment distinctly; I almost fell to my knees. "Congratulations, Miss Pillay. You are now officially a permanent resident of the United States." My heart was overwhelmed with gratitude. My hands shook and tears poured down my face. I looked up, and prayed in wonder, thank you, God! You have given me more than I could ever imagine or deserve!

After leaving the embassy and sharing my news, my cousin and his family took me to a popular seafood restaurant in Johannesburg to celebrate. I was honestly still in shock, so overwhelmed with joy at the opportunity I had been granted; I did not want the day to end. I could not believe that I was a permanent resident of the United States. This was so different from my time in the U.K. as now I did not have to worry about a visa ending. I could live in the U.S. forever. My mind raced with daydreams and possibilities of what living in America would be like, even silly and impossible things like meeting Oprah and Tom Hanks!

Within a month, I received my green card in the mail. I could not stop looking at it. I remember thinking, "It really is green." Staring at that card made the dreams that God placed in my heart so many years ago more real and possible than ever. For the first time, my dreams matched my reality.

I had to make an initial trip to the U.S. to complete the final paperwork before moving there permanently. I flew nineteen hours from Johannesburg to Atlanta, Georgia, where I completed my point of entry process before continuing to my destination in Santa Monica, California where I had family. I had no idea how big the United States was, and thus I was shocked when the flight attendant announced our flight time from Atlanta to LAX would be nearly five hours.

This was my first flight on American Airlines. I took note of the flight attendants with their crisp uniforms and American accents. Flying across America on American Airlines almost seemed too good to be true. Everything seemed unreal, perhaps I should have asked the person in the seat next to me to pinch me! I could not believe my American dream was no longer a "dream."

Soon afterward, I returned to South Africa to gather my belongings and planned for my new life in the U.S. Family members threw me a beautiful farewell party. Many of them had not seen each other in over a decade, including one of dad's sisters, who had been very close to mum and had refused to speak to him after mum's passing. My farewell celebration provided a chance for them, and other estranged family members, to reconnect. They continued to stay in touch even after I set off for my new adventure.

Though I was obviously eager to start my life in America, saying goodbye to family and friends proved difficult. I had grown closer to all of them since we were reunited. To prevent my family from worrying, I lied that I had a job and a nice place to stay. I didn't want my dad to worry because he had his own financial stress and health issues.

At the airport, many tears were shed while my family gave me their blessings. My dad hugged me and gave his blessings with a proud smile. Everyone was proud of all I had achieved to this point, and they knew I deserved this special opportunity. A girl from Durban, South Africa, who struggled to even finish high school, was now leaving for the land of opportunity where dreams come true.

I knew very little about the U.S., but I had told a patient whose daughters lived there about my green card. He told me his daughters lived in Savannah, Georgia and that it was beautiful and affordable. So, I settled on Savannah, and searched the internet for available rooms to rent there. I conversed by email with a young woman who was a student at The Savannah College of Art and Design about an available room in the house where she had lived. Everything seemed to be falling into place, we agreed on the room, and she even offered to pick me up from the airport.

When I landed, the young woman who was supposed to pick me up was not there, so I called her from a payphone. It was the first time I had actually spoken to her, and I realized quickly her English was not very good. She told me she was unable to pick me up and gave me an address of where to go. I called a taxi to take me there, and shortly the driver was pulling up outside the university. I got out nervously and waited. I was somewhat relieved when I saw a young Asian woman walking toward me; she was accompanied by an older woman who would turn out to be the house's landlord with the room for rent. The landlord was suspicious of me, coming to America all on my own.

I remember thinking that if she said no, where would I go? It was getting late, and I could not afford a hotel for more than a week. I showed her all my papers, but she was not happy that I did not have a confirmed job. She was more concerned if I could afford the rent. I showed her my few hundred dollars and offered to pay her two months' rent in advance, desperate for her to say I could come to the house. I had no other options. After much questioning, she agreed to rent me the room. I felt such a sense of relief, knowing I had a roof over my head.

It turned out that the room I had rented had no furniture, so I slept on the floor. My roommate gave me a thin blanket, and I used three layers of clothes to keep me warm. The next day I went to the dollar store to get a few supplies. I also tried a corn dog for the first time; it was not my favorite, but it was cheap and kept me full. For days that turned into weeks following my arrival, I would spend most waking moments searching for jobs, but with little luck. My phlebotomy certification was not valid in the U.S., so I was looking for any possible job. I decided to take a bus and walk through the city, hoping to find a "Help Wanted" sign posted in a window. I went to a few hotels that needed room attendants, filling out applications and waiting for a response.

After three weeks, I was getting worried, so I paid a recruitment agency to find a job for me, figuring this would be the solution. I should have read the fine print; I did not understand that a job was not guaranteed. They sent me job openings, and I had to apply. I had used most of my food money to pay the agency. Fighting a battlefield of doubt in my mind, I began to wonder if I made the right choice in coming to America.

It dawned on me that I possibly could put my prior caregiving experience to use. I decided to sign up on Care.com, an in-home care matching service, and almost immediately was offered a live-in position with a military family in Gulfport, Mississippi. The wife had temporarily lost oxygen to the brain during childbirth, and it had left her with brain damage. I was quickly running out of money and took the job. The husband flew me down to live with them and care for his wife. While this family was good to me, I knew from the outset that it was just temporary. I needed to do something else to achieve my college education goals.

They were moving back home to Dallas, and he offered me to go with them. I appreciatively declined knowing I wanted a different path. I used my last paycheck for a flight to California, knowing I could go to my granny's brothers and their families in Santa Monica. It would be good to be close to family again. Once in California, I secured a job at elder care residential facility in Santa Clarita. I could live at the facility, too, which solved the problem of finding a place to stay. I managed the care of six elderly residents. It was a job I knew how to do, but living there meant I was always on call, and the work exhausted me. I was not strong enough to lift the patients when they would fall, and my back was constantly in pain.

One night, I had an anxiety attack. It felt like a heart attack. I got scared, which made matters worse, and ultimately called the paramedics. I was rushed to Henry Mayo Hospital, where my heart rate and blood pressure were dangerously high. I was admitted for the night. I remember a hospital staff asking me for health insurance, but I had to tell her I had none. She asked if I could make at least a portion of the payment, but I had barely any money after buying my ticket to California. Regardless, everyone at the hospital was kind to me and helped calm me. I felt bad that I was not able to pay.

Once discharged, I called a taxi to take me back to the facility and was put back to work immediately. I knew I could not continue in this stressful environment, but I had free accommodation, and I needed to send money home to dad. Both dad and my stepmother were unemployed, and dad's health issues were getting worse.

The niece of one of the residents I cared for noticed how heavy my workload was and offered a place to stay with her and her wife. I accepted their offer and living with them was like having two mothers. They were so kind to me.

I secured a new job as a caregiver at Summerhill Villa Senior Care and then a second job at Sunrise Senior Living, earning minimum wage at both. I worked at one facility from six in the morning until noon, and then went to the other from one in the afternoon until nine in the evening.

I loved caring for the residents. I saw my mother and father in all of them and caring for them was a blessing to me. The knowledge and wisdom I received from them were priceless. They encouraged me, and they taught me many valuable lessons: to appreciate my time with my family and friends; to educate myself to the highest possible level; to take time to do things I enjoy and to always take care of myself. They showed me it was important to be open to change because two things in life have no guarantee: love and life itself. They encouraged me in things of the heart, teaching me that I would know if a man was "the one," and to let love find me. Sharing time with the residents showed me that every day is a blessing, and not to rush life but rather live gracefully. These words of wisdom taught me to see life with grateful eyes.

One evening, I was in the cafeteria talking to a co-worker about my goal to achieve a college degree. She advised me on various options and opportunities. I previously did not know anything about student loans and scholarships. She helped with the applications, and I was thrilled to receive a student loan and scholarships which would enable me to pursue a bachelor's degree.

Since I had been a young girl, I had dreamed of becoming a nurse like my mother. But when it came time to declare my major, I had a change of heart. I decided on psychology. I wanted to understand the diseases of the mind, gain insight into mum's suffering, and hopefully help others burdened by depression. I decided it would be a greater honor to mum if I could help any of the millions of people thinking of suicide. I believed helping people to see a reason to live, and giving hope to the lost and broken, would be the best way I could honor her life; a life that could not be saved.

Since I could not afford a car, nor did I have any credit history to secure a loan for one, I took the bus to my two jobs. I had no free time, but the sacrifice was worth it. This was my chance at a future.

My day started at four in the morning, running to the bus stop to catch the 4:55 bus at Rue Entrée. The route was twenty minutes by car, but it took an hour and thirty minutes by bus. At least I could use this time to work on my assessments. After a day of work and classes, I would catch the 10 p.m. bus and didn't reach home until 11:30 at night. This was my daily schedule, and my weekends were dedicated to school studies. I sat in my room for long hours, trying to get ahead of my syllabus just in case I needed to work overtime at one of my jobs. Statistics was my weakness in college, and every time I looked at my assignments for that class, it flooded me with anxiety. Slowly, I learned to take motivation from all the things I was good at, and I approached statistics with a positive mindset and overcame my fear of numbers.

I remember moments of exhaustion with work and school, but I really could not find a reason to complain. I was living with a wonderful family, and I was finally getting my college degree. These were the moments I had longed for, and my heart was filled with gratitude.

Many immigrants like myself are searching for their own "American dream." Just one "yes" for a green card, job offer, college admission, or many other such once-in-a-lifetime opportunities can be the gateway to accomplishments that would not otherwise be possible. Though, I have learned the American dream does not come easy; it takes hard work and dedication. My granny always told me, "Hard work killed nobody, so keep going!"

We must use the tools at hand to start and stay true to the course set before us so that our aspirations clear away the obstacles of fear. Keeping my eye on the end goal kept me inspired; even though the fires of life in my youth threatened to pull me down a different course, I stayed focused and found my way. My American dream came with many hurdles, but sometimes in life, we must go through a difficult-albeit amazing journey to get to where we are supposed to be.

"No matter where you are from, your dreams are valid."
- Lupita Nyong'o

19

GOODBYE, DAD

It was 2013, in my final year of undergrad studies, and Christmas was approaching. Though every year thus far I had gone back to South Africa for the holidays, this year was to be different. I wasn't able to get the time off of work to make the long trip home. Dad was saddened I would not be home for Christmas, but I assured him I would be home at the end of January. I even showed him my confirmed plane ticket during a video call.

A few weeks before my visit to South Africa, I was on the bus to work when I received a call from my uncle. It seemed odd; my family never called me much, rather mostly communicated by text. I was not at work long when one of my "mothers," the ladies I lived with, came in looking for me. I was setting the table for residents to eat lunch, and I was surprised to see her at my workplace. When I saw her walk toward me, I felt a sense of uneasiness. Her eyes were teary, and I could immediately recognize the look of grief on her face. As she walked toward me, fear arose. All I could think of was my father. Before she could say anything, I blurted out, "Is it, my dad?" She didn't need to respond; I knew he was gone.

I fell to the ground in tears. I broke down in front of the residents and staff. My manager helped me to a chair to try to console me. My body was in shock, and I could not stop shaking. I kept asking, "What happened? Are you sure he is gone?" I went home and began receiving calls from family back home with the full story. My father had been shot in a carjacking.

Dad had secured a minibus and made a small income by transporting people to church and other venues. It was January 17th. He and my stepmother dropped off a few people at church and decided to stop at a park to eat lunch in the van. Dad heard a sound. He walked around the back of the van and found a man staring him down. My father was police trained and armed, but while his focus was on this man, another came from behind him and shot him in the back. Perhaps the criminals tried to rob him as well, but he had no money to take; they fled immediately. My stepmom went to dad and held him as he breathed his last breath.

I was on the phone with my family all night. I kept hoping for a miracle, even though I knew dad was gone. I was worried about my sister. I was angry at that moment for many reasons, but there was one thing that made me scream with anger: my family was still forced to be at the scene of the incident. My father's body was lying on the hard cement ground in the pouring rain for over five hours. Because it was a crime scene, they could not move his body. The crime in South Africa is appalling, and it is not unusual to wait hours for assistance. My family waited for government services to take his body to the mortuary. I saw my father's picture on the front page of our local newspaper, his body covered as he lay on the hard ground in the heavy rain, and his white sneakers peeking out. That image vividly stayed with me for a long time.

I immediately booked the flight back to South Africa. Fortunately, I was always a careful saver and could afford the ticket home. My emotions vacillated between sorrow, anger, and confusion. I asked God, "Why? Why must I go through the pain of losing a parent again?" I could not stop crying.

It was early in the morning when, I started my journey to LAX, consumed by emotions. Usually I loved flying, but this time I could not imagine being on a plane for nineteen hours. I just wanted to be back where my father was. I prayed to God to give me strength and rest. During my flight on Delta Airlines, the flight attendants were so gracious to me. They invited me back to the galley to sit with them in a quiet place where I could have more privacy. Their compassion, kindness, and empathy made the trip bearable. I could not thank them enough as I exited the plane.

I deplaned in South Africa and paused before walking through the glass doors into the terminal. I knew what was ahead after I walked through those doors: the grim reality that my relatives would be there to greet me without my father. When I walked into the terminal, I was overwhelmed by relatives embracing me and welcoming me home. My uncle hugged me tightly and said with resolve, "I am your father now." It made me feel safe and grounded.

The love and support of my family made me stronger every day. My father had left instructions in his will for me to be the sole person to make decisions about the funeral. I told myself: You need to be strong for your father and give him a respectful and honorable farewell, no matter how difficult it is.

The days that followed were filled with decisions and errands. It was very hard, but my uncles were there to support me. I was strong until I asked my family to take me to the spot where my dad was killed. I fell to the ground in grief at the spot of his final moments alive. I pictured the whole scene as described to me and from what I had read in the local newspaper. I placed a cross on the ground while my family laid flowers around the cross. I said a prayer of thanks to God for bringing my father and me back together and restoring our relationship. I had five years of good memories with him, after many years without, that I would keep alive in my heart. I said my final words to him and prayed that he and mum were together.

On the day of dad's funeral, we began with the Indian tradition of allowing immediate family members to be alone with the deceased before proceeding to the church. My uncle came to ask my sister and me if we wanted our time with him. My sister, who had found it hard to make peace with dad, spoke tearfully, "Yes, please. I want some time alone with my father. There are a few things I wish I would have told him." My heart broke for my sister and her pain. I knew she needed this time to begin to heal.

I thought of the day at the airport when God showed me dad's heart and set me free. I was so thankful I forgave him and could rebuild a relationship in the short time God had given me with him. I smiled inside thinking about our father and daughter pool competitions, late nights watching war movies, and fascinating talks about untold mysteries. I grieved his loss, but I had no guilt or regret. I knew I had done everything I could to make him proud and happy.

People often ask me how I could forgive my dad after everything he did to mum, my sister, and me. It is not easy to forgive, but who am I not to? I have made many mistakes myself. I know it was also only possible through God, showing me that forgiving my dad and letting go of bitterness was the only way to my own healing.

The police attempted a preliminary investigation into my father's murder, but they had no leads. I was angry to think there would be no justice for my father's death. I briefly went back to the U.S. packed up some stuff, and arranged for a temporary leave from school and work. Then I returned to South Africa for six months, determined to find my father's

murderer. I interviewed neighbors and friends, asking
whether dad had any grievances or owed anyone money. I
would frequently go to the police station, asking if they had
any leads. I have no doubt that I frustrated them. Once a
police officer turned to me and said, "If you bring me a lead,
I will work on it!" I revisited the site of his murder over and
over again and stewed in my anger.

I also prayed to God for clarity, realizing I had brought
my whole life and the future I had been working toward to
a standstill. I wanted to believe that dad's death was more
than a random attack. I carried the wound of a daughter
who lost her father to a carjacking, but in reality, crime was
so rampant in South Africa that a daughter or son lost a
parent to violent crime virtually every day. I accepted that
nothing could bring dad back to me, and I knew I had to let
it go. My father would have wanted me to return to the U.S.
and complete my degree, and it was time for me to chase
my dreams.

Many times, I have thought about how I missed going
home for Christmas that year. It was another time of
questioning, 'If only I had...' My flight to visit home at the
end of January had already been booked before Christmas
had even come. Who would have known that I would need
to book a flight before my planned travel time to bury
my father? I regretted not being home for Christmas and
sometimes believed that if I had been home on January
17th, he would not have been at that park.

The reality is that our thoughts of, 'If only I had stayed,' or 'If I had just been home for Christmas,' do not change anything. We must believe we were at the right place at the right time, even when tragedy befalls us. Acceptance is found in letting go of what you could not control. Believing it could have been different only leads to broken roads of confusion and disbelief.

"After climbing a great hill, one only finds that there are many more hills to climb."

\- Nelson Mandela

20

A GRATEFUL HEART

Back in California, I dedicated myself to my studies and earned my bachelor's degree. I walked up to the stage with many emotions flooding over me. As I received my degree in hand, I raised it and looked up with tears dedicating that moment to my parents. I always wanted to make them proud, and I did my best to live a life that would honor their memory.

This accomplishment and every sacrifice that I've made along the way, was for my future and my beloved parents. There was a time in my life that finishing high school was the most I could hope for, and now here I was graduating from college in the United States! The impossible dream had not just become possible; it had become real. And I was invigorated by what other possibilities were to come.

After graduation, I traveled to Oahu, Hawaii, for a dear friend's wedding. It was there where I had met a charming man named Luis Felix.

Felix, as I call him, was a chef. We exchanged emails,

and he asked me for a curry recipe. After a month of daily emails, Felix mustered up the courage to ask for my number. He would message me every morning and evening. I looked forward to Felix's messages and genuinely enjoyed his company. I really liked Felix but did not expect to have the opportunity to come back to Hawaii again, so I did not imagine anything would come of it.

Upon my return to Southern California as a recent grad with a psychology degree, I began my search for a paid position in suicide prevention. However, every job I wanted was a two-three hour commute. Then, out of the blue, I got a call from American Airlines with an offer to interview for a job as a flight attendant. Two years prior, a friend from college worked as a flight attendant, and I started considering it as an option. The few flights taken in my life left a huge impression on me, from the flight attendants who cared for me while traveling to dad's funeral, to those lifting me out of my past and into new opportunities in the U.K. and America. So, I had applied with American Airlines but almost forgotten that I had until hearing from them a couple of months after graduating.

It had been such a long time since I had applied, and now that I had my college degree, I was no longer interested. I'd thanked the man on the phone but told him that I wanted to look for work in my field. He left his direct number and told me to call if I changed my mind. I kept thinking about the job and the adventure of traveling the world. Perhaps it would give me the chance to explore, have fun, and maybe even see Felix again.

Felix and I had been chatting by text, and I really enjoyed our friendship. I called American Airlines back, and arrangements were made to come for an interview in Dallas. I got the job on the spot and, within a few months, started intensive eight-week training.

I had gone from hesitation to being extremely excited about this new opportunity that seemed to drop into my lap. I had always admired flight attendants with their crisp, elegant uniforms and always what seemed to be genuine kindness toward travelers. I wondered where I would have been without the aviation industry. Flying had given me the ability to spread my wings. After all, it was airplanes that had taken me to the places where I've found personal growth and opportunities to make my dreams come true. Never stop believing in your dreams, no matter how far it may seem. Small steps are better than no steps, and everyone's journey is unique.

> *"An African heart with an American dream."*
> \- Michelle Felix

21

FINDING LOVE AGAIN

The intensity of my flight attendant training made college-even statistics-almost look easy. It took me entirely out of my comfort zone, a soft-spoken girl having to run emergency drills and shout evacuation commands. During my final emergency drill evacuation testing, I had failed. My anxiety got the better of me, and I was at a loss for words during one of my drills. My instructors looked back at me with hope and tried to encourage me, but I could not move or talk. I walked away with my head lowered, and I could see the watery eyes of my instructors. I was devastated that evening, thinking all those weeks of intense training could be for nothing if I did not pass my final attempt.

The next day, during class, my instructor called out my name, and as I stood up, the class clapped and cheered for me. "Go, Michelle!" they shouted, "You've got this!" I walked with my head up, and I was ready. One chance is all you need, Michelle, I told myself. Boldly, I approached the S80 aircraft door, believing in myself and God giving me strength and clarity; I performed my best evacuation drill ever. My instructors cried and held me tight. All my classmates gave me a standing ovation. I was officially a flight attendant for the world's largest airline. Who would have thought this could be when just a few years ago, on my first plane ride to the U.K., I was too timid to even ask the flight attendant for water even though I was parched.

Felix continued to call and text to encourage me. By the end of my flight attendant training, I had found a new dimension of myself as boldly confident and almost extroverted. At the time that we had first met, Felix was in a desperate time in his life. He had come out of a bad relationship and had been numbing his pain with heavy drinking. Felix told me that he would sit on the beach and cry out to God to send him an angel or someone he could love who could help pull him up from this lowest point of his life. He felt that God had answered that prayer by sending me to him.

As we got to know each other better, I finally began to share more of my personal story with Felix. It was difficult for me to open up about it. I had lived most of my life reluctant to talk about mum and the circumstances of her death and events that followed. While working on my undergraduate in psychology, I had learned the importance of emotional regulation as well as validating and expressing your feelings. What I had learned in school helped me express and manage my emotions. I slowly began to talk about my life events, first to Felix, then to friends and co-workers. I realized that every time I shared my story to encourage others, I was healing, too. I was finally able to talk about mum and dad without breaking down or feeling uneasy.

Felix couldn't understand how I could be so happy after everything I had been through in my life. I told him that the world can give temporary and conditional happiness, but only God can provide joy that is everlasting.

My flight attendant graduation was coming up, and Felix insisted on coming even though I told him hardly any of the other flight attendant trainees had friends or family coming. I knew he genuinely cared for me when he used his last $800 for a plane ticket to be with me for a forty-minute ceremony. Our relationship continued to grow, and I would visit him on my days off in Oahu, Hawaii.

I proceeded cautiously through the relationship, and we fought at times as he struggled through his healing journey. Felix's daily and excessive use of alcohol presented a big obstacle for us. He used alcohol to escape his pain, but it negatively affected his work, lifestyle, and our relationship. On New Year's Eve, I gave him an ultimatum; I told him we couldn't move forward in our relationship and he would need to control his drinking or get help if we were to be together. December 31, 2015 was the last day any alcoholic substance touched his lips. I saw God working in his life and refining him.

Felix's consistent honor and affection toward me opened my heart to love and be loved in a way I did not know was possible. He prayed every day for God to make him a better man. He believed that was what I deserved, and so that is what he wanted to become. Felix showed me more love than I had ever known in my life. He will tell people that I made him a better man, but I will quickly add that it was all God.

I remember our first real date as if it were yesterday. Neither of us had much money. I just came out of unpaid flight attendant training, and he just started a new job. We were both hungry and wanted to get something to eat, but he was afraid to ask me what I would like to eat because he only had ten dollars. We saw a Taco Bell, and since we both loved tacos, we knew that would be our designated date spot! We had a feast with the one-dollar meals—a good spread of soft tacos, refried beans, and sodas. I was sublimely happy with this first date meal, and I loved that we could simply be ourselves. No filters, just two real people from humble beginnings and contentedly dining at Taco Bell.

We would spend most of our time on the beach. Felix surfed for hours while I would read a book. We were quite different people. He loved the outdoors, mostly the water, and I could not even swim. He loved riding his motorbike, and I could not ride a bicycle. Felix loved sushi, and I loved curry, though we shared a love for rum-raisin ice-cream.

We were different, indeed, but we found ways to enjoy things together. Respecting each other's differences and not expecting the other to change themselves was the key to our successful relationship. We both learned from each other and grew together. Felix taught me everything about island life, and I taught him everything about the Indian culture.

After a six-month courtship, he proposed to me on my birthday at Lava Lava Beach Club in Waikoloa. We were staying in a cottage on the ocean next to the restaurant. There was a live band that night, and they started to play our song, "Thinking Out Loud" by Ed Sheeran. As my eyes were fixed on the beautiful ocean waves, I shouted out, "Our song is playing!" and turned around to see Felix down on one knee, with a cake in one hand and a ring in the other. We both had tears in our eyes as he asked for my hand in marriage. My answer was a one hundred percent yes! We almost dropped the cake as we laughed with joy. Everyone at the restaurant, including the band, started clapping and cheering. It was a day I will never forget. I had found the one my soul loves.

On January 17, 2017, the day my dad took his last breath of life, we got married in a small ceremony on Hawaii Island, where we made our new home together. I have always believed in celebrating one's life with joyful moments. Entering this new beginning was my way of honoring my father's life.

We did not have a car, just a 390 KTM motorcycle. He wore a suit, and I wore an Indian red attire. We climbed on the motorcycle, ready for this new chapter in our lives. We must have been a sight to see, a bride and groom cruising through the island on a motorcycle, especially with my red and gold Punjabi flying everywhere. It was like a real-life Bollywood scene. Felix had asked me if he should rent a car, but I told him no, that the best thing we could do was just to be us, especially on the most important day of our lives.

We rode home and had a kebab cookout on our lanai. Looking at the beautiful red sunset over the ocean, we held hands and thanked God for each other.

> *"Love is the humblest yet the most powerful force that the human being has."*
>
> - Mahatma Gandhi

22

GOING HOME

While my family was happy to hear the news of my marriage to Felix, they could not help but feel a little uneasy. They did not know this man who had captured their Michelle's heart. We planned a trip to South Africa so Felix could meet my family and see my treasured homeland. My family wanted to see us get married and be apart of the celebration. We couldn't afford a full wedding, so I spoke to my family about a small church ceremony that the family could be part of. However, my family had something else in mind to send us off into this new chapter of life.

Both of my parent's families decided to combine efforts to give us an amazing wedding celebration. My aunt and uncle opened their home for the pre-wedding festivities. The night before the wedding there was a huge family reunion filled with laughter, dancing, and lots of cooking and eating. Chef Felix made a beautiful feast including a bountiful salad with his signature dressing and lamb rack with Caribbean style couscous and vegetables. Boy, did he ever impress my family with that meal! They had already fallen in love with him the first day they met him, and his delicious food was the icing on the cake.

That same night after dinner, my aunty came to me and presented me with a beautiful gold necklace that had belonged to mum's mother. I cannot put into words what it felt like to hold this stunning piece of jewelry in my hands, something that had belonged to someone I had lost. The necklace and epaulets were the only material items I had that were connected to mum. It was to be such an incredible honor to wear that necklace on my wedding day and feel my mother close to me. When I thanked my family for their generosity, they told me that if my parents were alive, this is what they would have done for me.

Keeping to the night before the wedding tradition, Felix and I stayed apart — he stayed with mum's brother and I stayed with dad's brother. Felix celebrated with my uncles until late into the night, and I stayed up with my aunties discussing funny marriage tips and making roti, a scrumptious Indian flatbread.

The morning of the wedding was very emotional for me. I was thinking a lot about mum and dad, wondering how this day would have been if they were here. I pictured my mum in a green saree running around making tea for the guests, and dad outside setting up the fire to cook the biryani (a delicious Indian mixed rice dish with meat and spices). Putting on my dress and taking pictures with my aunt, cousins, and sister lightened my spirit. The time was coming close, and I had no idea what to expect as my family had told me no details about the wedding, they had planned for us.

The church ceremony was very emotional and almost surreal. There was a moment to pray and light candles in honor of my parents. I walked down the aisle with both mum's brother and dad's brother. My family members wept sweetly as the pastor announced our union.

After the ceremony, we headed to the reception at the Gateway Hotel, Umhlanga. Everyone was inside the ballroom, waiting for our big arrival as Mr. and Mrs. Felix. Our favorite Bollywood song "Sajda" played, and, as we entered, neither of us could hold back our emotions as we saw inside. We walked into a red and gold palace fit for royalty. Our hearts were overwhelmed with gratitude. It was more than we could ever ask for or imagine. We had a beautiful and joyful night of Bollywood dancing, laughter, and making new family memories. It was beyond anything we could ever imagine or afford; it is a day Felix and I will cherish forever.

A few days later, my uncle and aunt blessed us with the most amazing honeymoon gift: a safari at the Nambiti Game Reserve. I was born and raised in Africa, but I had never seen the "big five" native animals: lion, leopard, rhino, elephant, and buffalo. Our safari days started at five in the morning to watch the animals feed. It was about fifty-five degrees Fahrenheit in the back of the open Jeep, but our excitement kept us warm. Seeing a hippo with his family watching us with suspicious eyes was priceless. The tiger that strolled around the Jeep with her cub made us uneasy, but she was only marking her territory.

One of the highlights for me was seeing a rhino. We did not see any during our daily tours in the Jeep, but on our last day at Ndaka Safari Lodge, I woke up early to take in the fresh air of the motherland. Suddenly, I saw an animal moving near my gate. I got a little closer and saw that it was a rhino. Overwhelmed with emotion, I cast aside any fear and started running toward the gate. I just needed one moment with this majestic creature. The rangers spotted me running and started yelling and screaming, "Don't get too close!" In all my excitement, I did not adhere to their warnings. As I got close to the rhino, I looked into her deep eyes and felt so much pain. I felt as though she was trying to tell me something and was compelled to get closer. At that moment, I saw God's heart in His creation, this gorgeous creature. She was so beautiful and massive; I felt honored just to be in her presence. The rhino walked away, but looked back at me once, and I smiled with joy. That feeling was something I will never be able to adequately explain.

Felix and I left the motherland with so much gratitude and emotion. I touched the ground and thanked God for the soil of Africa.

*"Africa-my beginning, my roots, and the soul of
my existence."*

- Michelle Felix

*"Dedicated to every wildlife that lost its life from the cruelty
of poaching. May the fight against poaching never cease,
for the value of life is the same across all living things."*

23

HEALING IN THE SKIES

Felix and I came back to the U.S. continuing our respective jobs as a chef and flight attendant. I enjoyed my job and was blessed to travel to beautiful places, experience different cultures, and establish lasting friendships. My career as a flight attendant made me bold, brave, and confident in my own skin. Every time I wore my uniform, it made me feel like I could take on the world. Now I understood the sparkle and poise mum had when she wore her nurse uniform.

The best part of my flight attendant career was the lasting friendships I had made. During long international flights, what we called "jump seat therapy," was part of the journey. I would sit with my fellow flight attendants in our jump seats, talking about our life journeys and sharing words of wisdom. On a trip to Santiago, Chile, I shared my story with a group of flight attendants. Upon hearing all that I had experienced, they insisted I write a book or make a movie about my life! At first, I laughed the thought had never occurred to me. We all have a story to tell. But it struck me that my story could be a way to encourage others, and it gave me a new perspective on using what I had been through to help others heal.

On our flight back home from Santiago, one of my co-workers told me she had called her mother after holding sixteen years of resentment toward her, that I had inspired her to let go of the anger and initiate the call. She said it was tough at first, but her mother's overwhelming joy at hearing her daughter's voice immediately dissolved my friend's fears. I was stunned at how our simple "jump seat therapy session," could spark a flame of healing and reconciliation.

The hardest part about being a flight attendant was being away from home so much. On months when I was on reserve, sometimes I was gone two weeks at a time, and it was hard to go that long without seeing Felix. I had long, sixteen-hour commutes flying round-trip between Dallas and Hawaii almost every week. For my first two years as a flight attendant, I was only home on the weekends. Eventually, it began to take a toll on my body, but coming home always revived me. It felt so good to sleep in my own bed and spend time with Felix. Many flight attendants make the sacrifice of not being home for the holidays, and I was one of them. Though I had not yet spent a Christmas with Felix, I loved creating Christmas festivities in January or birthday celebrations when we could fit them in. Every time

I had returned home from a flight; Felix would be waiting at the airport with a lei to welcome me.

We both felt it was worth it in the beginning. We had the flexibility for it, and we got to travel many places together. We ate authentic cuisines and soaked up rich cultures, colors, and flavors. I felt it was a privilege to experience different cultures and observe and embrace the lives of others. We've made incredible friendships, all the while exploring mother nature in all her beauty, glory, and power. Traveling created beautiful memories and seeing the world from the eyes of others is something I will always treasure.

One of the most important lessons I've learned during my time as a flight attendant was the power of words and a supportive presence. On one occasion, I was working a typical late-night flight. I had finished the service and was eating my own dinner in the galley. I heard someone crying but could not tell the nature of the cry. Were they sick? Upset? In need of help? I rose from my jump seat to see where the cry was coming from, and I spotted a passenger in the second to last row in the middle, sobbing and wiping his tears. I could tell he was embarrassed, having passengers on either side of him and crying in this way. At that moment, I remembered my flight to South Africa to bury my only remaining parent and the way the flight attendants had comforted me and provided me a quiet place to grieve. I had never been good at consoling people. I had such a tendency to be shy and was always scared I would say the wrong thing. I felt an overwhelming need to console this man, but I did not know how.

Before I could muster the courage to move toward him, another flight attendant went and asked if he would like some space and privacy. The man shook his head no. Seeing him sitting alone in his pain brought back so many emotions for me. I could not help myself, and I walked up to his row, reached over, and gently placed my hand on his shoulder. I said to him, "Whatever you are going through, it's going to be okay." He looked up at me with gentle eyes as he wiped his tears. Before he exited the plane, he came up to me and hugged me. His voice cracked as he said, "I really needed to hear that. Thank you." At that moment, I was struck by how powerful our words can be and how merely truly acknowledging someone's pain can bring so much healing. Sometimes, we just need to hear, 'It's going to be okay.'

This memorable moment also taught me the power of kindness. You don't have to do extraordinary things to be kind. Sometimes, just a smile, good morning, or a gentle touch of encouragement can make a difference to someone's day. I will never know why that young man was crying, but I pray my simple words of encouragement gave him a glimpse of hope. Being kind costs nothing, yet it has the power to change lives.

"Our spoken words have the power to heal. Speak words of life."

\- Michelle Felix

24

NEW BEGINNINGS

F elix and I decided it was time for us to buy a home. It was a stepping stone for us to build our family. Not knowing anything about purchasing real estate, we attended home-buyer seminars to increase our understanding. Our budget was tight, and it looked like the most we could afford would be an apartment or condo, less than a thousand square feet. After a long search for properties within our budget, we found a condo. It was a simple home with much work needed, but it would be ours.

We were overjoyed, and I immediately started thinking of ideas to make it feel like home. We were ninety-nine percent through the process, and we even got an email congratulating us as first-time homeowners. We started packing and celebrating until we got a call notifying us that we did not get approved for the loan.

Our hearts were broken, and I was angry with God. I came to God with my frustration, asking why he would build up my hope only to let me down? After this tremendous disappointment, Felix suggested that we hold off on buying a home for a while, as it was causing too much stress. At first, I thought that was a good idea. Maybe it just was not our time. But it was nauseating to spend $1,700 on rent every month for our studio apartment, and not be building equity. So, Felix and I turned our focus to building our credit and began to work hard to pay off debt. The dream of having our own home was ever present still, but we knew we needed to improve our finances first.

When Felix's mother's birthday rolled around, we decided to go visit her. It would be a nice diversion, and I was excited to finally meet his parents. We had created some beautiful memories together and Felix got to see his beautiful mother after twelve years. During the five-hour flight back to Hawaii from Los Angeles, I looked at a realtor app and saw a beautiful ocean view condo within our budget. It seemed unbelievable that there could be a condo with an ocean view and more space for the same price as the one we had submitted an offer on before.

As soon as we landed, we called Jenni. She was truly God sent, even crying with us when we did not get the last home. That day she had looked me in the eye and promised she would make us homeowners one day. She genuinely loved helping young first-time homebuyers. Upon our return from Los Angeles, we climbed on our motorbike with our heavy backpack and headed straight from the airport to the address on the listing. Jenni was there waiting for us, but there were two families viewing the place as well. They both seemed extremely interested.

We walked into the condo to see a panoramic ocean view, and my heart fell to the ground. I stood on the lanai and took in the beautiful view. Afraid of being disappointed again, I asked God, is it possible? I felt a sense of calm come over me, as if God was telling me, "This is your new home." I did not look any further than the view and told her, "This is the one." She rushed to the office to draw up the paperwork to seal the deal. Within three weeks, Felix and I found ourselves standing in front of the door with my hand shaking as I turned the key to our new home.

It is so important to trust in God's timing and not our own. The disappointment we felt at losing our first home when we were in the final days of closing was crushing. As it would turn out, God had something so much better for us; better than anything we could have ever hoped for or expected through our perspective. It is human nature to want things in our own time. However, one closed door can lead to the perfect open door. God wanted to give Felix and me a dream home beyond our expectations. We just needed to stay true to course, do the work, and persevere.

As soon as we moved in and got a few essentials for the home, my next goal was finding a furry, four-legged best friend. I searched for months to find the right dog. The island did not have many boxers. I joined the Boxer Club of Hawaii Facebook page and prayed that God would send the right pup my way. I was on a trip for work, away from home for weeks, when I got a message of a boxer litter born in Ocean View down on the south end of the island. Within hours, Felix was in Ocean View to put down a deposit. We had to wait seven weeks to bring him home. I could not wait to see him. My heart skipped a beat when I first saw "Felix Junior." He was perfect in every way, and our home was now complete.

I had treasured my childhood memories with my three amazing boxers, never forgetting them. And I had promised myself that one day I would have another boxer to honor Mash, Tiffany, and Jock. Memories came flooding back of happy times playing with my dogs, as well as the pain of losing them all. Loving and caring for our puppy provided another milestone of redemption. I could not save Tiffany from abandonment and ultimately her merciless death and saying goodbye to Jock had felt like giving away my best friend. I have always seen my furry friends as more than dogs. There were times in my childhood when my parents could not see the ways the tension at home was affecting me. Yet Mash, Tiffany, and Jock seemed to be able to see right through to my pain and knew exactly how to comfort me.

I wanted to honor my childhood dogs and all they gave to me by giving Felix Junior the best possible life. Felix Junior looks identical to Tiffany, and, extraordinarily, he was born on the anniversary of the day of mum's death. God was truly showing me all the ways that love can heal. Seeing

Felix Junior is a constant reminder of how Tiffany, Jock, and Mash cared for me. To me, Felix Junior is more than a dog or our pet; he is part of the family.

Felix and I both loved motorbikes, especially since it was our main means of transportation. Felix decided he would teach me to ride a motorbike, and what a journey it was! At age thirty-seven, I didn't even know how to ride a bicycle! So, we started with that. I fell a few times at first, so Felix decided to get me training wheels. It honestly was a hilarious sight: a grown woman riding a tiny bicycle with training wheels. There were many basic things in life most girls learn about which I did not get a chance. I suppose I was preoccupied trying to survive. I was grateful to Felix for his patience and persistence in helping me learn this new skill.

It took me three days of practice to finally learn to ride a bicycle. I then went to motorcycle school so that I could get my license. I passed the written test, but on the first day of practice testing, I dropped the motorbike and injured myself. The instructor stopped me and told me that for my own safety, he couldn't allow me to continue. I was extremely disappointed. Felix had invested so much time in helping me learn, and I wanted to make him proud. I went home, and, with great sadness, I told him I didn't pass, and I didn't think I would ever get my license. He looked into my tearful eyes, and said, "You will ride a motorbike tomorrow." Felix and one of his close friends came to support me the next day as I got back on the motorbike to practice. It was a long day, but no one was leaving until I rode off into the sunset!

Today, Felix is sometimes my passenger as I drive the motorbike, and we enjoy the beautiful island on two wheels. The truth is that I did not know how to swim, ride a bicycle, or drive a car until my mid-thirties. There was no one to teach me these things when I was growing up, and my fears always got the better of me whenever I thought of attempting them on my own. What I know now, is that we are never too old to learn anything. Everyone's path in life leads them down different roads. The road set for me was a long one with detours, twists, and turns, but I eventually got there. It is not always the destination that matters; it is the journey.

Felix and I were building a happy home with Felix Junior in our beautiful condo. But I knew there were still more dreams yet to reach and decided to go back to school for my graduate degree. I had doubts that I could complete the challenging curriculum, as I had never viewed myself as an intelligent person, just a hard worker. I was so scared of failing especially after learning what the tuition would cost us. My husband believed in me more than I believed in myself and encouraged me to take a leap of faith; I registered for graduate school.

All my free time went to my courses and studies. Once again, I was back in a rigorous schedule of balancing work and school. I commuted eight hours from Dallas to Kona weekly, and on those commuting flights, I would pray for an open row so I could stretch out all my books and notes to work on my assignments. Those long flights helped me navigate my master's program. Felix always supported me too, working extra hard around the house. I would always come home to a clean house, laundry done, and dinner made. Felix wanted me to put all my energy into school. His love and support in this time made a world of difference.

It was challenging work, but I pushed myself to the limit. Every time, I felt I did not have the strength or understanding, I would think of mum and it reminded me of why I needed to be strong and press on. I wanted to be just like her, a woman who educated herself against the odds and created a life and a career to serve others. Before the separation, mum talked about furthering her studies. She was my role model, and I wanted a similar future for myself, but I also wanted to be stronger than her for her. I wanted to live my life by running after everything she did not have the chance to do. I wanted her weaknesses to become my strengths, and honor her life by being a brave, courageous daughter.

In March of 2019, I received my graduate degree in psychology. I had the incredible honor of my aunt and cousin from South Africa attending my graduation. On the morning of graduation, my aunt cried telling me, "Your mother would have been so proud of you." There were many joyful tears shed that day. I had tried my best to make something of my life, and it was profound to think that I had made mum proud. I received my diploma that day in memory of mum's unfinished graduate degree. The journey is complete, mum; I said silently as I walked across that stage.

Around the same time, I decided to apply to become a U.S. citizen. I had come to the United States eight years prior with big dreams that God had placed in my heart. There were many times when my American dream seemed impossible, but dreams are worth fighting for. Nelson Mandela once said, "Education is the most powerful weapon you can use to change the world." I seized every opportunity I could to work toward my dreams.

It was such a tremendous honor to attend my citizenship oath ceremony in Honolulu, thinking back on the journey that had gotten me there. I was profoundly grateful for all the opportunities the U.S. had given me. America truly is a land of opportunity where dreams can come true if you chase them with dedication and hard work. As I spoke the oath that would make the United States my permanent home, I knew I would never forsake my humble beginnings in South Africa or the many opportunities America had given me.

Within the span of just a few months, this once frail, insecure, and broken girl had earned her graduate degree and U.S. citizenship. I marveled at the expanse of God's grace.

My journey, though difficult, had brought me to this point. Through it all, hope gave me the courage to believe in dreams, forgiveness gave me the power to heal, and a higher love set me free.

"Envision where you see yourself, stay focused, and press on."

\- Michelle Felix

25

2020

The year 2020 was one none of us will never forget. Only a few weeks into the year, dynamics started shifting across the world: lost jobs, lost homes, and even so many lost lives. Due to the COVID-19 pandemic, the airline industry became very different as well, and suddenly the career I had loved for so many years became a source of fear. Though I had grown much stronger physically over the years, I still knew that my chronic asthma made me vulnerable to the virus, and when I was away on flights, Felix could not rest until I was home safely.

The commute from Dallas to Kona also became a challenge with fewer flights coming into the island, which meant that the chances of being furloughed became increasingly possible. Saddened by the situation, and not knowing how long our world would be plagued by this new threat, I decided to be proactive and started looking for other jobs.

Felix got laid off in March, and jobs were scarce, especially chef jobs with tourism slowly deteriorating on the island. We had also lost our catering business which was a side company we built together to bring in extra money. We had loved the opportunities our catering business gave us to cook for private functions and make connections in the community. The pandemic seemed to be stripping away everything we loved doing; it was as though a dark cloud had rolled in over us, just as it had so many others. Both Felix and I were wired for hospitality and serving people; it was our comfort and joy as much as it was the source of our livelihood.

Though I had started looking at other possible job opportunities, I pushed myself past my fear and continued to fly because I felt I needed to help Felix and maintain some form of constancy amidst all this abrupt change. He was going through a very dark phase in his life, and I did not want him to feel burdened about being unemployed. The pandemic was worsening; people were dying in the thousands every day around the world. With so much confusion, unrest, and lives lost, Felix's concern for my health was growing. I would tell him people still needed to get places, particularly getting home to their families. He replied, "Nothing is worth more than your life." I hung up my wings, understanding it was a necessary end, but still sad to see this season of my life end.

Unsure of what the next chapter would bring for Felix and me, we both decided it was time to reinvent ourselves. Unemployment benefits would run out soon, and jobs were limited. The uncertainty and tension in the world were impacting our little home, but we felt strongly there must be some reason or purpose for us to be in this situation. We needed to ask God the right questions. That sense created an awakening that shook all our senses.

I had always wanted to work with vulnerable youth, having had an unstable childhood myself. I wanted to use my academic achievements and life experiences to encourage, inspire, and give children hope for the future. When I saw the job listing, I knew I had to pursue it. I applied and got the job. The role focused on providing safety and support for youth impacted by trauma, and it called upon virtually every experience I'd had in my life – from my own family experiences, to working with the children of Umtata, to the knowledge and understanding I had obtained through my studies. In the middle of a global pandemic, God had placed me in the position I was meant for: guiding and advocating for vulnerable children. Now, I have the privilege every day of making a difference in the lives of these children.

I also decided to further my education and added school back into my schedule. I signed up for a graduate certificate in Applied Behavior Analysis, to become a board-certified behavior analyst. I have always been fascinated by human behavior, and the specialization would help to deepen my understanding. Education has always been a source of empowerment for me; it is truly life-changing. We all have our passions in life. My passion has always been to follow the example of my mum and educate myself to the highest degree possible because there is truly no end to learning.

The year 2020 would bring even more change to our family. One night, Felix received a revelation from God about his future. As much as the culinary field was his passion, he'd realized that it was time for something new. Felix started researching new digital trends and spent three months building up his knowledge through training programs. He would wake up at three every morning, motivated and focused on reinventing himself to provide for his family. He completely shifted careers from chef to a digital professional, creating live cooking videos to spread the joys of cooking. He would say, "You can take the chef out of the kitchen, but you can't take away one's passion."

Perhaps a global pandemic, with so much worry, suffering, and uncertainty in the world, is an odd time to change careers completely. However, Felix and I knew it was time to change our focus, believing there must be a reason for the circumstances around us. It was the ideal time to hold on to the good things, be grateful for the smallest of things, and bolster our faith in humanity by caring for one another and giving our earth a chance to heal.

One of the most crucial lessons the pandemic has taught me is that we can't always reclaim what we have lost, but we can try to restore, rebuild, and use these times to reflect and find inner peace. Some of the most powerful life-changing events in history have occurred from tragic circumstances. Let us come out of this with new horizons, a second chance, and a whole new meaning to life.

It was also during the pandemic that I decided to listen to the suggestion that my family and friends had given me years earlier and write my story. I began to put my thoughts and emotions into words, hoping that sharing my story would shed a glimpse of hope and healing for others.

There have been so many moments in my life when God delivered me from pain only to have the brokenness of the world bite back with more rejection and heartbreak. Every healing moment brought me greater clarity, peace, and strength. Little by little, God remade me.

Learning to love myself and the love from my husband, pets, family, friends, and the indescribable love of God pulled me out of my brokenness and made my heart whole again. I know love has healed me in many ways. When all else fades, love still stands because nothing is more powerful than love itself.

"As long as love exists, we can heal."
- Michelle Felix

CLOSING

never had the opportunity to say goodbye to my parents, but the little memories I have of them live stronger in my heart more than ever, even as time wears on. Sometimes, we can find peace simply in the memories we have of the loved ones we have lost, knowing we were loved by them and remain grateful for the time God gave us with them, even if that time was limited. My parents certainly made mistakes, but it never changed their love for my sister and me. I will never take for granted the privilege of knowing them, loving them, and creating lasting memories with them.

During my early teens, I was ashamed of my life. I avoided making friends and was scared to talk about my broken family. And to now find myself publishing my story for anyone to read is remarkable to me.

At times I felt like my mind was a battlefield, fearful of an uncertain future with no understanding about the loss and pain that had transpired in my past. I've chased answers and acceptance until I realized that peace would not come from certainty. Peace is something we must find for ourselves by laying down our heavy burdens.

I am no longer ashamed of my past, and I am grateful to all those who took me in and did their best to care for me for short seasons or long. My past has helped me become the person I am today. My journey has made me stronger; my failures have made me wiser, and every painful moment has given me a perspective of gratitude. If you are struggling with despair or desperate for hope, please believe me that healing is possible.

So often in our lives, we wish to go back and change individual decisions we've made. We do not have the power to change yesterday, but we can use today to make things right or at least make them better. Through my healing journey, I realized that learning to forgive yourself is perhaps even more difficult and more important than finding forgiveness for others. By letting go of heavy burdens buried deep inside, we begin to experience acceptance and love, and the healing comes with it.

Looking back on my mum's desperate need to be loved by my father and my longing for love in an unhealthy relationship, I have realized we should never depend on anyone for our own happiness. Find your own joy, whether it is dancing in the rain, writing a song, traveling the world, playing a sport, or simply being happy with your own company. There is so much life can offer; you just need to find what makes you smile. Falling in love and sharing your life with someone is a beautiful gift to enhance your happiness, not be your reason to live or be happy. Find what makes you happy and love yourself.

The world is not always going to be fair. Instead of turning your pain into anger, let your pain help you rise above the clouds and soar into new possibilities. Let your pain inspire you to be the light and turn your pain into something fruitful and good.

Though there were many moments of uncertainty in my life, I marvel that even the darkest times didn't stand in the way of pursuing my dreams. I have always remembered God's grace in my life and that every season has been held in His hands. Even when I was led through the fire, God was closer than no other. I know with certainty that I have lived in the mercy of God.

I am so incredibly grateful for my journey. Every heartache and every painful moment have given me grateful eyes. If I had the chance to do it all over again, I would not change a thing. I am who I am today because of my experiences. Knowing and fulfilling your purpose in life requires living and walking your own unique path. Better to fail in your journey than to try to live another man's journey. We must not attempt to chase the paths set out for others; we create our own roads and walk them as though we own them because we do. Your life experiences are your own—no matter where you are in your journey right now, just remember you are created with purpose and perfectly made.

If this book can encourage, inspire, and give hope to just

one person, my purpose in putting these experiences into words has been achieved.

"One's journey to a whole heart begins with healing from within."

\- Michelle Felix

DEDICATION

In honor of my parent's Subbammah & Somasunthus Pillay.

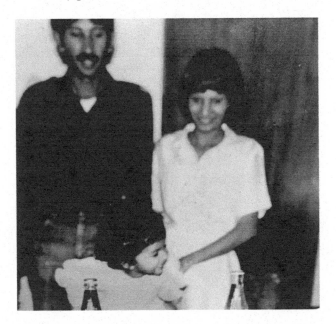

I've always thought I could save you, but now all I can do is honor you. To my courageous and selfless mother, the first woman in my life to provide me safety and comfort, the woman I had longed to become- you are the one for whom I live to make proud. To my brave father, the first man in my life, my protector and teacher- thank you for supporting me in all my endeavors. I will always be your little girl. Please forgive me, my parents, for always needing you to be there. I know now that our individual journeys were uniquely created and guided by our God. For each step of each of our journeys, I will forever be grateful.

AUTHOR BIO

 Michelle Felix was born and raised in Durban, South Africa. She moved to The United States in search of a better life. She works as a human service professional and lives in Hawaii, Whole Heart is her first book.

"Remember your resilience in the face of adversity.
You are stronger than your greatest fear."
- Michelle Felix

www.michellefelix.life
www.thefelixs.com